THE MEANING OF LIFE AT THE EDGE OF THE THIRD MILLENNIUM

by

LEONARD SWIDLER

Paulist Press ♦ New York/Mahwah, N.J.

Library of Congress Cataloging-in-Publication Data

Swidler, Leonard J.
The meaning of life at the edge of the third millennium/by Leonard Swidler.
p. cm.
Includes bibliographical references.
ISBN 0–8091–3315–6 (pbk.)
1. Religion. 2. Religions. 3. Ideology. 4. Christianity–Influence.
I. Title.
BL48.S925 1992
200—dc20 92–10911
CIP

Published by Paulist Press
997 Macarthur Boulevard
Mahwah, New Jersey 07430

Printed and bound in the
United States of America

CONTENTS

I. DOES LIFE HAVE MEANING?

Does life have a meaning? First, a question to the question: What is the meaning of "meaning"? Or, What are we intending to ask when we want to know the "meaning" of something? "Meaning" here indicates relating some "thing" to a "knower" so that the purpose of the object is understood by the knower. Or, put otherwise, "meaning" is the relating of an "object" to a "subject" in a way that the "subject" perceives the point, the purpose of the object (a "subject" is anyone with a knowing capacity, and an "object" is anything that is known). For example, if I, a "subject," know a computer in such a way as to understand its purpose, then I am relating it to myself in such a way as to grasp its "meaning." To a primitive tribesman, on the other hand, a computer would be "meaningless."

There are only two ultimate answers to the initial question, Does life have a meaning? The penultimate one, "I don't know," even though it may be the only answer some humans come up with throughout their whole lives, is basically unsatisfactory. Given the structural desire of humans always to know the answer to every question, such a non-resolving answer will ever be pushed toward a resolution. Many individual humans may never attain a resolution, but others of the same frame of mind will ineluctably continue to strive for resolution.

There are two possible ultimate answers to the question. One is, no. Human life is meaning-less, ab-surd. The problem with such an answer for humans is that it is fundamentally unacceptable to our nature, which has at its core the need to know—endlessly. Given the human faculty of knowing abstractly, that is, in a way that is not limited to any particular things, the object of our desire to know is open-ended. Now, to say that our whole life is without meaning simply means that we are unable to relate reality as we experience it to ourselves so as to see its purpose. Such a path persistently followed leads unavoidably to "malaise" (*Sickness Unto Death*, Søren Kirkegaard), "nausea" (Jean-Paul Sartre), "madness" (Friedrich Nietzsche), for such a way of thinking is "madness," that is, following the path of ir-rationality—the very definition of madness, in-sanity. Even those stalwart philosophers of existentialist thought who spoke of the absurdity of life, in the end urged humans to give life meaning themselves, claiming that such meaning cannot come from the outside, but only from within. Still, in the end, they too turned away from an utterly meaningless life to the brave forging of one's own meaning—otherwise, they said, beyond the brink lies the abyss of Sartre's *Nausée*, which is to be avoided at all costs.

The only other answer to the question of whether life has meaning or not is, yes. Life does have a meaning, or many meanings. That implies that reality as experienced can be related to the knower. It further implies that the relationship is such that it indicates some "direction" to the movement, the change, that takes place in human knowing, living and acting knowingly (beyond the physical animal nature of humans, these three elements are essentially what makes men and women human). It is right to speak of a "direction," a *telos*, to human experience, otherwise we say that our activity, our experience, is "pointless," is "purposeless." Life implies experience; experience implies change; change implies movement. Movement can be either "directioned" or "directionless," as in going back and forth or up and down. But in the latter case we say that such movement is pointless, meaningless. But "meaningless" movement has already been rejected in finally saying "no" to the answer which claims life is meaningless. Hence, to claim that life has meaning is to imply that it has a certain direction.

What then is the "meaning" of life, in what "direction" is it going? Each individual human must search for an answer to this question for her/himself. But since being human means to live in a network of relationships, the answer to this fundamental question is not found alone, but rather in community. The very way the question is posed by each human is something largely determined by the community in which she or he grew up, and hence the answers are also greatly influenced by the environment in which the questions are asked, by the categories in which the question and answers are cast, and by the mental and emotional horizons within which the whole enterprise takes place. All of these put together comprise what we normally call Religion, and the Culture that corresponds to it.

It is precisely that complex of ultimate questions and answers called Religion (and today in certain circumstances, Ideology—more of that later) that I wish to investigate. In this investigation I want to look into three things: First, I want to ask some basic questions about what Religion is; secondly, I want to look at what the relationship among the various Religions (and Ideologies) is, and needs to be, now at the edge of the Third Millennium; and thirdly, I want to ask what it is Christianity has to offer to the world at this critical juncture. The first two items seem obvious enough, but the reason for the third needs a little explaining.

On a personal note, I as a Christian naturally am interested in how Christianity can creatively relate to the world today, and I presume that is also true of other Christians, and even to some extent for the non-Christians who are affected by the actions of Christians. However, when these two groups of people are put together, because of the intimate relationship of Christianity to Western civilization and the present pervasiveness of Western civilization throughout the world, these two groups in effect constitute the whole world. Said other, Christianity has had—and in many ways continues to have—a massive influence on shaping Western civilization, which has brought the world to the point of existing within a "Global Culture"—which continues, of course, to sustain a plurality of regional cultures within it. Further, Christianity is also leading the world of a plurality of Religions out of the Age of Monologue into the Age of Dialogue, which has already begun now at the edge of the Third Millennium. Thus, Christianity is helping in a determining way to shape Religion in general, and hence, to provide all human life with meaning.

II. RELIGION (IDEOLOGY)—ITS MEANING

1. *Definition*

Scholars writing about the meaning of religion usually start by stating that it is not possible to give a definition of Religion, then often follow that up with quotations of a number of "descriptions" by other scholars, and end up nevertheless offering their own "description," or perhaps tentatively a "working definition." I am more optimistic about the possibility of giving a definition and offer one at the start:

> Religion is an explanation of the ultimate meaning of life, based on the notion of the transcendent, and how to live accordingly; and it normally contains the four "C's": Creed, Code, Cult, Community-structure.

Creed refers to the cognitive aspect of a religion; it is everything that goes into the "explanation" of the ultimate meaning of life. *Code* of behavior or ethics includes all the rules and customs of action that somehow follow from one aspect or another of the *Creed*. *Cult* means all the ritual activities that relate the follower to one aspect or other of the Transcendent, either directly or indirectly, prayer being an example of the former and certain formal behavior toward representatives of the Transcendent, like priests, of the latter. *Community-structure* refers to the relationships among the followers; this can vary widely, from a very egalitarian relationship, as among Quakers, through a "republican" structure like Presbyterians have, to a monarchical one, as with some Hasidic Jews vis-à-vis their Rebbe. The *Transcendent*, as the roots of the word indicate, means "that which goes beyond" the every-day, the ordinary, the surface experience of reality. It can mean spirits, gods, a Personal God, an Impersonal God, Emptiness, etc., etc.

Especially in modern times there have developed "explanations of the ultimate meaning of life, and how to live accordingly" which are not based on a notion of the transcendent, e.g., Marxism. Although in every respect these "explanations . . ." function as religions traditionally have in human life, because the idea of the transcendent, however it is understood, plays such a central role in religion, but not in these "explanations . . ." for the sake of accuracy it is best to give these "explanations . . ." not based on notion of the transcendent a separate name; the name often used is: Ideology. Much, though not all, of the following discussion will, *mutatis mutandis*, also apply to Ideology even when the term is not used.

It is clear when we say that Religion provides an explanation of the "meaning" of life, that therefore all Religion is constitutively related to humans; it is to provide *our* understanding of life. (The great Swiss Protestant theologian Karl Barth agreed with this idea when he argued that all Religions are human creations—and therefore will necessarily be misleading, he concluded—but then went on to insist that Christianity was not a Religion, for it, alone, was created by God, by the Transcendent, and therefore it alone was not misleading.)

Also apparent in this definition is that Religion offers an explanation of the "ultimate" understanding of life, not just part of it. It is an attempt to "get it all together," as the American expression has it. Religion does not just attempt to explain the meaning of physical life, as "bio-logy" does, or just psychic life, as "psycho-logy," or life in community, as "socio-logy," or the earth on which we live, as "geo-logy," etc., etc. Rather, it is an explanation of the meaning of Ultimate Reality and how Ultimate Reality relates to all finite reality, and most especially to us humans. Perhaps the best way in Western languages to speak of Ultimate Reality as Ultimate Reality relates to us is to follow the Greek linguistic tradition reflected in the other "logies" above: "Theo-logy." The ancient Greeks spoke of Ultimate Reality as *Theos*, God. Hence, Theo-logy basically means the study of *Theos* and the relationship of the rest of reality, especially humans, to *Theos*.

I am aware that the term theology is not only culturally a Western term, and therefore has severe limitations, but also that it is a term which has come to mean Ultimate Reality understood in "personal" terms, and therefore is still more restricted. Concerning the latter, I do not want to claim that Religion must have a personal understanding of Ultimate Reality in order to qualify as Religion; that is a matter which is a potentially fruitful subject of dialogue between theists and non-theists.

Concerning the former restriction, the fact is that no term from whatever culture can possibly be without its limitations. Hence, the best we can do is consciously to choose terms that we think will be the most helpful—and then always bear in mind their cultural and other limitations. Only thus can we avoid on one hand being condemned to silence, because we cannot find any words to describe reality which will not be limited and hence distorting, and on the other hand being guilty of "idolatry," that is, mistaking our words, the "idols" (i.e., the images, the symbols, the "finger pointing to the moon") for the reality they are supposed to describe, to image.

There is of course much more to reflect on concerning the various explanations of Ultimate Reality and the relation of humans to Ultimate Reality, all of which Religion is supposed to provide. Therefore, I mean to return to that subject later.

2. *The Way*

However, no one, West or East, would want to use the term theology, even with all the cautions outlined, as if it were synonymous with Religion. Religion is much more than just an intellectual explanation of the ultimate meaning of life—absolutely vital to Religion as that theoretical dimension is. Religion is also "how to live according" to that explanation. It is a "Way" of living, of life. This is reflected in the interesting fact that many major Religions of the world have the very term "way," or some variation of it, at the heart of their self-understanding.

For example, in the three "Semitic," or "Abrahamic," Religions—Judaism, Christianity, and Islam—all the following terms mean the "Way":

Central to Judaism, the Hebrew word *Halacha*, "the Way," has come to mean the Rabbinic teachings, the "legal" decisions to be followed, in order to lead a life according to the Torah, that is, as "instructed" by God (the Hebrew word *Torah* means "instruction").

At the beginning of Christianity the followers of Jesus (*Yeshua*, in Hebrew) were not called Christians, but followers of "the Way" (*Hodos*, in the Greek of the New Testament—Acts 9:2; 19:9, 23; 22:4; 24:14, 22) "Rabbi" Yeshua taught and exemplified.

In Islam the traditional way to live a correct life was to follow the *Shar'ia*, an Arabic term for "the Way"—specifically the path to find water in the desert; it also, analogous to *Halacha* in Judaism, came to mean the myriad "legal" decisions that should be followed by the devout Muslim.

Much the same is also true for the major Religions coming out of India—Hinduism and Buddhism:

In Hinduism there are three major "Ways," *Margas* in Sanskrit, to attain the goal in life: *Moksha* (Sanskrit for "liberation"), namely, the Way or *Marga* of knowledge (*Jnana*), the *Marga* of works (*Karma*), and the *Marga* of devotion (*Bhakti*).

In Buddhism the key term meaning "Way" is *Magga*, in Pali, and refers to the Noble Eightfold *Path* (the fourth of Gautama's fundamental Four Noble Truths) to be followed in order to reach *Nirvana*, the goal of life; moreover, Gautama himself in his first, fundamental, sermon, and Buddhism after him, described his way as the Middle *Way* (*Majjhima Patipada* in Pali) between harsh asceticism and loose sensuality which will lead to the goal of life.

For the major Religions of the Far East too, the term the *Way* was central:

The very name of Chinese *Tao*ism places the Way, *Tao*, at the center, at the foundation of the entire Religion, the goal of which was to discern the *Tao* of the universe and live in harmony with it.

This notion of the Way, the *Tao*, was also central to the doctrine of Confucius, who taught that "The Way of Humanity" (*Ren-Tao*) is to follow "The Way of Heaven" (*T'ien-Tao*)—for Confucius Heaven, *T'ien*, was largely "personal," *Theos*, though eventually, and especially for the Neo-Confucianists of the Song Dynasty (960–1279 C.E.) and afterwards, *T'ien* became largely nonpersonal.

Japan's native Religion, Shinto, likewise has embedded in its very name the term "the Way," namely, *To*, "The Way of the Gods," *Shin-To*. The term was taken from the Chinese with the same meaning, *Shen-Tao*, to distinguish the original Japanese Religion (which in pure Japanese was called the "Way of the *Kami* or Gods," *Kami-no Michi*) from that Religion of India, Buddhism, which came to Japan by way of China through Korea, also known in Chinese as "the Way of Buddha," *Butsu-Tao*.

3. *Goal of Religion*

The goal, or goals, of Religion have been described in many different ways. At times the goal seems to be quite crude, and at others it appears to be quite sublime. For example, on a rather primitive level, one goal might be to gain a self-benefitting power or to deflect an injurious power. Here Religion tends to merge with magic—or emerge from magic. On the other hand, on a higher level one goal of Religion might be to engage in self-less praise of Beauty, Truth, Goodness, or to pour one's self out for another. The Beatific Vision of Christianity would be an example of the first, and the Bodhisattva of Mahayana Buddhism an example of the second.

a) *Popular Religion—Reflective Religion*

This wide variation in goals underlines the importance of bearing in mind the distinction between popular level Religion and reflective level Religion. In popular Religion the degree of reflexive consciousness, of self-awareness, is quite low. It is rather like that of children experiencing something. Children are not very aware of their *experiencing* something, but rather tend to be exclusively focussed on the thing experienced. We thus say that children are *naive*, that is, their mentality is still close to the way it was when they were born, *natus*. Things tend to be understood by children in a fashion that is rather literal, straight-forward, im-mediate, that is, with no inter-mediate element, with no mental distance between the thing experienced and the one experiencing.

But as children grow through puberty into adulthood they gain a certain distance on the things they learned when they were young, and on themselves. They become reflexive, reflective. They become aware not only of the things they encounter, that they experience, but they become increasingly aware also of their *experiencing* of things. They often become critical of the things they had previously learned, at times rejecting them because they judge that they could not possibly be literally true, as they had earlier understood them to be.

If the process of maturation continues as it should, young adults will gradually move to the stage of a "second naivete," as Paul Ricoeur names it. Now adults realize that often those things they understood when they were children as literally true, and rejected as not literally true when they were young adults, are in fact true—far *more* true than the children who took them literally thought, or the adolescents who rejected them in the same way. Now they are seen for what they truly are—and they often are metaphors, symbols, images pointing to a much deeper reality than can be expressed in literal language.

Matters of deep human import are far too weighty for prose to carry them adequately; poetry—metaphor, symbol, image—must be brought into play to carry such a message, even partly adequately. For example, a prose description of one's beloved (blond hair, blue eyes, so tall, etc.) is much too feeble to express the object of such an important human experience as being in love; hence, the world is full, not of love prose, literal description, but of love poetry, which bursts with metaphors, symbols, images.

However, all this is true of the development not only of individuals, but also of whole communities, and indeed ultimately of the entire human race. We see the breakthrough to the level of "reflective Religion" particularly in what Karl Jaspers called the "Axial Age," a period in human development when the major world Religions in several different cultures were born. Humankind in general moved through a kind of "communal puberty."

Thus there will be individuals, regardless of age, whose religious consciousness is on a quite naive level, and those whose religious consciousness is on a very reflective level—and persons everywhere in between. There will also be whole communities of these different types; for example, certain Protestant Christian churches tend to be "fundamentalist" (naive) and others tend to be "liberal" (from the critical to the "second-naivete" level).

Some communities may even to a large extent be officially on the "second-naivete" level, but with much of its leadership still largely, or at least to a significant extent, on the "pre-critical" level; this is true at present of the Catholic Church with its Vatican II (1962–65) official commitments to an historical, dynamic, dialogical, collegial, freedom-oriented, turn-toward-this-world self-understanding on the one hand, and the static, pre-Vatican II, fortress mentality of Pope John Paul II and his chief advisers, like Cardinal Ratzinger, and many of the bishops John Paul II has appointed in the past thirteen years.

It is also important to keep in mind that one can hardly expect that the level of a person's religious consciousness will be higher than her or his general human consciousness; so, a person who in general is rather naive would also tend to be religiously rather naive. However, perhaps because religious institutions frequently are so old, and hence often very traditional and conservative, it is far too often true that many people's level of religious consciousness is below that of their general consciousness, especially in modern society with its rapidly expanding educational system, which tends to raise the general level of consciousness of whole populations. James Fowler, for example, judges that American churches and synagogues tend to cultivate their congregants at a level significantly below their level of moral and faith ability.[1]

b) *Terms Used*

There are many different terms used in the Religions of the world to describe the goal of Religion. These terms reveal an understanding of human nature, and of Ultimate Reality to which it is related, that is held by at least part of that Religion's tradition. Hence, it will be revealing for us to analyze, however briefly, some of the most prominent of these terms—perhaps in the end thereby permitting us to conclude with a consensus understanding of the goal of Religion in general:

i. *Redemption* is a term used in the Abrahamic, and other Religions—very prominently in Christianity—which etymologically means "buying back," "ransom." At times, however, both in the Hebrew Bible and in the New Testament, it simply means the "liberation" of humans. Although it is not always clear in the Hebrew biblical texts what humans are liberated from, both there and in the New Testament it usually is liberation from "sin," meaning from the condition of being in thralldom to the power of evil resulting from humans having committed evil acts. Humans are prevented by sin from attaining their goal, which ultimately is living in harmony or union with Ultimate Reality, that is, for monotheists, with God.

ii. *Liberation* (*Moksha* in Sanskrit) is a Hindu term describing the goal of life in negative fashion, that is, the freeing of the individual human self or soul (in Sanskrit, *atman*, "breath," which linguistically is related to the Greek word for breath, *atmo*—as in the English word "atmosphere") from a constant round of new physical lives (*samsara*, Sanskrit for "passing through," or "trans-migration"). Some (in fact, Bud-

---

[1] See James W. Fowler, *Stages of Faith* (New York: Harper & Row, 1981), p. 107; also, Leonard Swidler, *After the Absolute. The Dialogical Future of Religious Reflection* (Minneapolis: Fortress Press, 1990), pp. 195–199.

dhism as well as Hinduism uses the term *samsara*) describe this samsaric ring as being within a single human lifetime, but traditionally it meant a series of lifetimes that a single *atman* passes through until it attains liberation, *Moksha*, so that it can thereby accomplish its desired end, that is, union with Ultimate Reality —in Hinduism called *Brahman*.

It is clear that there is a close resemblance between the largely Hindu term "Liberation" and the largely Judeo-Christian term "Redemption." Both are a freeing of the inner "spirit" (which is simply a Latin-rooted word for "breath," *spiritus*) from that which prevents the self, the soul, from reaching its goal, which in both traditions is fundamentally the same: union with Ultimate Reality. How that Ultimate Reality is understood and what "union" with it means is variously explained—but more of that later.

iii. *Enlightenment* is a term most often found in Buddhism to describe the goal of life. Indeed, the very name of Buddhism contains the term Enlightenment: *Bodhi* in Sanskrit means "enlightened," and Siddharta Gautama (563–487 B.C.E.) was a *Buddha*, an "Enlightened One." At bottom, Enlightenment means the perception of reality, including preeminently one's self, as it truly is. Hence, Enlightenment is a human state of being which can be attained in this life.

Theravada Buddhism teaches that only a few can attain Enlightenment (or *Nirvana*, to be discussed further below)—and hence is called by those who disagree with it, *Hinayana*, or "Small Vehicle"—whereas *Mahayana*, "Great Vehicle," Buddhism claims many, or even all, humans can attain *Nirvana*. Japanese Zen Buddhism refers to this Enlightenment as *Satori*, and according to one sect, Rinzai Zen, it comes suddenly, whereas according to another, Soto Zen, it comes gradually. It should also be noted that this knowledge, this "Enlightenment," is not a theoretical kind of knowledge, but an experiential one which utterly transforms all subsequent experience.

iv. *Nirvana* is another term Buddhism uses (as does also Hinduism and Jainism from about the same time as the rise of Buddhism and Jainism, i.e., fifth century B.C.E., though in somewhat different ways) to describe the ultimate goal of human life. Literally in Sanskrit it means "blown out." What is blown out is the *Tanha*, the distorting "craving," which causes the *Dukkha*, "suffering" humans experience throughout life (because they unrealistically attempt to "cling to"—*Tanha*—things, even though all life is in reality transient, *Anicca*). When that state of *Nirvana* is attained, a person is then in a condition of blissful calm. However, as already has been mentioned, *Nirvana* can be arrived at only by perceiving reality, and most of all one's self, as it truly is. To some extent, this is like the view of the slightly later Greek thinker, Socrates (470–399 B.C.E.), who taught that ignorance is the source of human evil.

v. *Heaven* as the final goal of human life is a term that has been prominent in the Judeo-Christian-Islamic tradition. In fact, however, the term appears in many religions, coming from more primitive times when the heavens above were seen as the source of light, heat, and life, and hence the abode of the gods—whither humans then also wanted to migrate. In popular religions of all kinds—not just the three Abrahamic ones—heaven became a *place* of bliss where humans went after death; the same localizing misunderstanding of heaven also happened to the Buddhist notion of *Nirvana*—in popular Buddhism it too became a *place* of bliss where humans went after death.

On the reflective level, however, as Jesus stated, "The kingdom of God [or, "heaven"[2]] is not here or there; it is *within* you (*entos hymon*—Luke 17:20). Clearly for Jesus, and subsequent reflective Christianity (and the same is true for reflective Judaism and Islam), heaven as the ultimate goal of life is not a place to go to after death, but a state of being, which is to be attained in this life—which, however, does not cease at the grave. In fact, the customary English translation of the New Testament *Basileia tou Theou* as "Kingdom of God" is really a mis-translation, reflecting the localizing tendency of popular

---

[2] The Rabbis of Judaism spoke similarly in Hebrew of the *Malkut Shomaim*, the "Kingdom (or better, Reign) of Heaven" (Heaven is a euphemism for the name of God), and this is reflected in the use of "the Reign of *Heaven*" by Matthew, the most "Jewish" of the evangelists.

Religion. It is more accurately translated as the "*Reign* of God," that is, the state of being wherein one lives entirely in harmony or union with God, which state of being should exist now, and continue after death.

Medieval Christianity combined this understanding with Aristotelian philosophy and described the ultimate goal of human life as holiness in this life and complete union with God after death, when humans will be "face to face" with God, utilizing to the fullest their highest human capacities, the intellect and will, in knowing and loving THE Truth, Goodness, Beauty, Being (which are various aspects of the Infinite Ultimate Reality of God) in what Thomas Aquinas calls the *Visio Beata*, the "Beatific Vision."

vi. *Communism* is the "final" state humanity is expected to arrive at in the historical future, according to Karl Marx and his subsequent theorists. In that situation there will be the "withering away of the State" because the new "Soviet Man" will have evolved and the force of the State will no longer be necessary; then will be fulfilled the "communist" goal wherein everyone will "give according to his ability and take according to his needs." Before that time the penultimate condition, Socialism, will have to be enforced through the "dictatorship of the proletariat."

Whether Marx himself held this position literally or not has been debated by subsequent Marxists, but clearly most of the "orthodox" variety (that is, those who took power under Lenin and Stalin and maintained it in the Marxist world until recently) did hold such a position, despite obvious contradictory evidence in Marx's writings. Thus, except to naive "orthodox" Marxists, it is evident that the condition of "communism" lies beyond human history, as an always receding horizon.

"Non-orthodox" Marxist thinkers have argued this cogently from Marx's writings, as, for example, Roger Garaudy when he was a member of the Politbureau of the Communist Party of France in the 1960s: "Yes, man will always be capable of an always greater future. For us, Communism is not the end of history, but the end of pre-history, man's pre-history which is made up of the jungle-like encounters common to all class societies. 'This social formation,' Marx writes in his 'Contribution to the Critique of Political Economy,' 'constitutes . . . the closing chapter of the prehistoric stage of human society.' "[3]

vii. *Salvation* is a term that is widespread especially in the Abrahamic Religions, but it is also one which can be used in regard to the final goal of humans in most, if not all, religions:

It should be noted, however, that Salvation is used both in its primary and secondary senses in religions. Its primary meaning is literally living a "whole, healthy" life. The term comes from the Latin *salus*, "health," whence a number of English and Romance language cognates are derived, all fundamentally referring to health: salutary, salubrious, salute, salutation. The Germanic counterpart is *Heil*, "salvation," and as an adjective, *heilig*, "holy," whence the English cognates: health, hale, heal, whole, holy. To be "holy" means to be "(w)hole."

The secondary meaning of salvation is "saving," that is, as when a "savior" rescues someone in danger of losing his/her "health," as, for example, when "saving" a person from drowning—whether in water or in "sin." Thus, even in its secondary meaning, the term "Salvation" ultimately means attaining, preserving or restoring a healthy, holy, whole human life—however understood.

Some religions emphasize the secondary meaning in claiming that "wholeness," "(w)holiness," can be attained only through the help of the "Savior." For example, in traditional Protestant Christianity, a person can be saved only thus: *sola fide*, "by faith alone," *sola gratia*, "by grace alone," through *solus Christus*, "Christ alone"; in Pure Land Buddhism calling on the name of Amida Buddha is the only, and certain, way for *anyone* to attain *Nirvana*: *Namu Amida Butsu*, shortened to *Nembutsu*, "Praise to Amida Buddha"). This way of being saved is described in Japanese as *Tariki*, "Other-power," in contrast to *Jiriki*, "Self-power."

Faced with the generally human religious question of

---

[3] Roger Garaudy, *De l'anathème au dialogue* (Paris: Plon, 1965); *From Anathema to Dialogue* (New York: Herder and Herder, 1966), pp. 90f.

whether humans are "saved" by either *Jiriki* or *Tariki*, it appears to me that here the traditional Protestant principle of *sola*, "alone," is not appropriate, but rather the Catholic principle of *et . . . et*, "both . . . and" is: On the one hand, *we* can become as authentically and wholly human as is possible for *us* only if *we* persistently and wisely make the necessary effort. But on the other hand of course we can attain success in this lifelong endeavor only to the extent that we have been *given* the wherewithal: If we had not been born, we could not become (w)holy human; if we die too young, if we did not have loving care in infancy, or if we did not have a good education and training, encouragement, love, moral example, inspiration, and on and on, we could not become (w)holy human according to our inborn potentialities. So, we become (w)holy human by both *Jiriki* and *Tariki*. But we must remember that when we speak of these two "powers" we are speaking on two different levels of causality. As a consequence, there can be no clash—only complementarity.

What it means to be authentically and wholly human, and the best way to attain such, however, is precisely where the greatest, most fundamental, divergences among religions appear to be found. As a consequence, it is important to reflect, however briefly, on the major ways of understanding what it means to be human. I will approach this question by looking at the fundamental ways of understanding human nature: human nature is a) fundamentally good, b) fundamentally corrupt, c) fundamentally mixed. Then I will offer d) a resolution of my own, after which e) an excursus on a contemporary understanding of human nature will be added. Many examples could be proffered, but it will be sufficient to allude to only one or two representatives of each fundamental view of human nature.

4. *Human Nature*

a) *Human Nature Is Fundamentally Good*

In the ancient world of the East, one of the strongest proponents of the idea that humans by their nature are good was the great Confucian, Mencius (Meng Tzu in Chinese, 371–289 B.C.E.). He argued that humans commit evil only because they forget their original good nature. The human who does evil is like a hill side that was covered with trees (i.e., with virtue, with instinctive goodness) which has been deforested by saw-toothed vice. That is, that person has been so abused by vice that s/he even can no longer discern her/his own instinctual spontaneous tendency toward altruism and justice: as, for example, anyone seeing a child about to fall into a well would instinctively rush to prevent it.

In the modern, eighteenth century West, Jean-Jacques Rousseau represents well the optimist tradition. For him humans are born good, but are corrupted by "civilization": "Man is born free, and everywhere he is in chains!" According to Rousseau, humanity's problems would be solved if the education of the young were such as to "lead out" the goodness inherent in the child, as the very term education, "*e-ducere*" suggests, and keep the corrupting influences of "civilization" at bay.

b) *Human Nature Is Fundamentally Evil or Corrupt*

In the ancient East a much younger contemporary of Mencius, the Confucian Hsün Tzu (c. 313–238 B.C.E.), took the exact opposite position of his elder and argued that "the original nature of humans is evil."[4] He was very detailed in his description of the innate evil tendency of humans: "Man, by his nature, at birth lusts for profit . . . is envious and hateful . . . and because he follows these tendencies, impurity and disorder result."[5]

In the post-medieval West, the sixteenth-century Protestant Reformers stressed the fundamental corruption of human nature after its sinful "Fall" in the "mythic" paradise of Eden.

---

[4] *Hsün Tzu—Basic Writings*, trans. by Burton Watson (New York: Columbia University Press, 1963), p. 157.

[5] *The Works of Hsün Tzu*, trans. by H. H. Dubs (Taipei: Confucius Publishing Co., 1983), vol. *Man's Nature Is Evil.*

Fallen humanity's state is so dismal, according to Luther and Calvin, that it can do nothing at all to attain its true goal, union with God. It can be "saved" only by God's free gift, *sola gratia*; and that comes, as noted above, only by faith in Christ, *sola fide, solus Christus*. Humanity's inability to do anything for itself was so thoroughgoing for Luther, that he taught that humans have no free will, and for Calvin, that he taught that each human's ultimate fate was predetermined, predestined, ahead of time by God, regardless of what the individual allegedly freely chose to do.

c) *Human Nature Is Fundamentally Both Good and Evil*

For Catholic Christianity humanity was created good (following the biblical Genesis story of creation, where the Hebrew original says that when God looked over his creative handiwork on the sixth day of creation he saw that it was all *mod tov*, "very good"), but through humanity's disobedience in the Garden of Eden it fell into a state of "Original Sin," that is, its intellect was darkened, its will was weakened and it developed an inclination toward evil.

Concerning the posing of the problem as Luther, and particularly Calvin, did, namely, asking about the relationship between God's omnipotence or complete foreknowledge—Providence—Thomas Aquinas, and Catholicism following him, steered between Scylla and Charybdis thus: "All things are subject to divine providence, but rational creatures are so in a superior way. For they are under divine providence by participating in it, for they are called to in some way *be* divine providence for themselves and for others."[6]

Thus, Catholicism taught that human nature was originally fundamentally good, but had been so stricken that it needed a "savior"; at the same time, however, each person must also

---

[6] Thomas Aquinas, *Summa Theologiae*, I-II, Q. 91, a. 2: "Inter cetera autem rationalis creatura excellentiori quondam modo divinae providentiae subiacet, inquantum et ipsa fit providentiae particeps, sibi ipsi et aliis providens."

freely collaborate with God's freely offered help, grace. Hence, humans attain the goal of life, union with God, not through faith alone, but through "faith *and* good works."

d) *Human Nature: Love of Self and Others Mutually*

As "balanced" as the Catholic "both-and" position appears in comparison to the Protestant "only," the terms in which the question to be answered was posed caused Catholics endless logical problems (not to speak of the immense intellectual antinomies Protestants ran into):

For example, how can one affirm both an Absolute Ultimate Reality, an Ultimate Uncaused Cause of everything—and at the same time a radically free human will (which of course must be the cause of its own decisions; otherwise it would not be free)? The difficulty, it seems to me, is the result of posing the question badly. If I ask, for example, How far is yellow? of course I will receive a non-sense response. So here, too. Christian thinkers in this matter were actually doing something even more irrational.

They were dealing with two elements, both of which by definition cannot be rationally "comprehended," namely, God (the In-finite cannot be "com-prehended," by the finite), and the free human will (if it could be "rationally" understood, it would then be "determinable" by reason—and therefore not radically free); then they had the *hubris* to ask how they were to understand the relationship between these two elements, neither of which they could understand. This is like trying to solve a mathematical equation with three unknowns—and no knowns!

I would like to offer an alternative description of human nature as found in its beginning and development in each human being, which I hope will be both true to our universal human experience and at the same time avoid the antinomies that the above traditional solutions ineluctably run into as a result of how they pose the issue:

What differentiates humans from all other living beings is the fact that they are animals with the ability of abstract thought, who therefore can become reflexive, and, as a result of this capacity, possess the ability of free choice (also called "love"). All our faculties of knowing—our cognitive faculties, mainly our senses and abstract intellect—present us reality under the aspect of "the true." All our faculties of desiring—our appetitive faculties, mainly our physical and emotional "drives" and our will—relate us to reality under the aspect of "the good."

The cognitive faculty moves outwardly and then inwardly, reaching out and drawing the outside world to itself by *knowing* it, and thereby "becoming one" with it; the appetitive faculty also moves outwardly and then inwardly, reaching out and drawing the outside world to itself by *loving* it, and thereby "becoming one" with it. To restate the latter: the nature, the very structure, of the appetitive faculty is to reach out toward what the cognitive faculty presents as true and good, and to draw it to itself, thereby becoming one with it; thus the fundamental meaning of the term *love* is, having perceived the good, to reach out and to draw it to oneself.

When humans are born they do not even know themselves as different from the rest of reality, but learn to know themselves only by coming to know "the other," as, for example, infants' coming to know their own fingers as different from the flame when they learn to know the flame by touching it. Thus as children develop they gradually become increasingly aware of their own selves and of others.

There is a similar mode of mutuality that operates in the appetitive, the love, area. Infants begin by perceiving the good—their mother's breast, for example—and naturally draw it to themselves, and in that sense "become one" with it. When they perceive the good, they will identify with it in one way or another—the natural manner for the appetitive faculties to operate. If in the process of growing up they receive much love, children will necessarily perceive the one loving them, their "lover," as the source of pleasure, as good, and will therefore reach out to their "lover," identify with her or him; their "lover" will also become their "beloved."

When the sense of identity with the beloved becomes strong enough, we speak of an "other self," an *alter ego*. Then in the natural process when a person's appetitive faculties perceive the good and draw it to its self, to its *ego*, s/he will also tend to draw the good to its *alter ego*. If the love identification of the "*primus ego*" with the *alter ego* is strong enough, more and more of the perceived good will be drawn to the *alter ego* rather than the *primus ego* (e.g., the father giving food to his child rather than keeping it for himself), possibly even to the extreme of "giving up one's life for one's friend"; and, as Jesus said, "greater love than this has no one" (John 15:13).

Thus, the very nature of humans is to love the good as it is presented to them, and their "greatest good" (because the most "human," most "humanizing") is to have others act in a loving way toward them—with which "other" they would then naturally identify, making the other to a greater or lesser extent *alter egos*, "other selves," thereby drawing the perceived good to them as well as—or even, instead of—themselves.

It should be noted that there is operating here something like a psychical version of the physical law of inertia: "a body at rest remains at rest, unless moved by another body already in motion." Humans would not perceive other loving humans as their "greatest good" were they not first loved by those other humans. That is, they would "remain at rest" were they not first "moved" by the "motion," the loving action, of the other, and hence in turn find them good—and therefore love them in return.

But how does it all get started? Ultimately "Ultimate Reality" has to be ultimate not only as a goal, a final cause (a *telos*), but also as a beginning (a *protos*), an efficient cause (*causa efficiens*). Process philosophers speak of Ultimate Reality as this initial efficient cause by its acting as a lure, a "Divine Lure." The New Testament says much the same when John remarks that, "We love because God first loved us" (1 John 4:19).

It is doubtless the awareness of the humanly natural movement from the *primus ego* to the *alter ego* that has led the great religious traditions to phrase their fundamental principles accordingly. For example, for both Judaism and Christianity the second of the two "great commandments," and the main way the first one is de facto observed, is "to love your neighbor *as* yourself" (Leviticus 19:18; Matthew 22:38). One begins with an authentic self-love, which then extends to the neighbor, the *alter ego*.

It must also be remembered that it is precisely by this mutual knowing and loving that humans develop their humanity ever more fully. It is the nature of humans to be potentially open to all being, cognitively and appetitively, as far as their faculties can reach—and they can always reach further. Humans are by nature "open-ended." In other words, humans fulfill their nature by a *process* of constant self-transcendence, a going beyond themselves, knowing and loving ever more "being"—and a convinced theist would add, ultimately knowing and loving "Infinite Being," the "Ground of Being," "Being Itself," called God.

The same principle of mutuality that starts from the center and moves outward is phrased in another way in most of the world religions in the various forms of the "Golden Rule":

> Perhaps the oldest recorded version—which is cast in a positive form—stems from Zoroaster (628–551 B.C.E.): "That which is good for all and any one, for whomsoever—that is good for me . . . what I hold good for self, I should for all. Only Law Universal is true Law" (*Gathas*, 43.1).

> Confucius (551–479 B.C.E.): When asked, "Is there one word which may serve as a rule of practice for all one's life?" he said: "Do not to others what you do not want done to yourself" (*Analects*, 12.2 & 15.23). Confucius also stated in a variant version—likewise in negative form: "What I do not wish others to do to me, that also I wish not to do to them" (*Analects*, 5.11).

> The founder of Jainism was Vardhamana, known as Mahavira ("Great Hero"—540–468 B.C.E.); the various scriptures of Jainism, however, derived from a later period: "A man should wander about treating all creatures as he himself would be treated" (*Sutrakritanga* 1.11.33). "One who you think should be hit is none else but you. . . . Therefore, neither does he cause violence to others nor does he make others do so" (*Acarangasutra* 5.101–2).

The founder of Buddhism was Siddhartha Gautama, know as the Buddha ("Enlightened One"—563–483 B.C.E.); the various scriptures of Buddhism also derived from a later period: "Comparing oneself to others in such terms as 'Just as I am so are they, just as they are so am I,' he should neither kill nor cause others to kill" (*Sutta Nipata* 705). "Here am I fond of my life, not wanting to die, fond of pleasure and averse from pain. Suppose someone should rob me of my life. . . . If I in turn should rob of his life one fond of his life. . . . How could I inflict that upon another?" (*Samyutta Nikaya* v.353).

The Hindu epic poem, the third-century B.C.E. Mahabharata, states that its "Golden Rule," which is expressed in both positive and negative form, is the summary of all Hindu teaching, "the whole Dharma": "Vyasa says: Do not to others what you do not wish done to yourself; and wish for others too what you desire and long for yourself—this is the whole of Dharma; heed it well" *Mahabharata*, Anusasana Parva 113.8).

The deuterocanonical biblical Tobit was written around the year 200 B.C.E. and contains a negative version—as most versions are—of the Golden Rule: "Never do to anyone else anything that you would not want someone to do to you" (Tobit 4:15).

The major founder of Rabbinic Judaism, Hillel, who lived about a generation before Jesus, though he may also have been his teacher, taught that the Golden Rule—his version being both positive and negative—was the heart of the Torah; "all the rest was commentary": "Do not do to others what you would not have done to yourself" (*bTalmud*, Shabbath 31a).

Following in this Jewish tradition, Jesus stated the Golden Rule in a positive form, saying that it summed up the whole Torah and prophets: "Do for others just what you want them to do for you" (Luke 6:31); "Do for others what you want them to do for you: this is the meaning of the Law of Moses [*Torah*] and of the teachings of the prophets" (Matthew 7:12).

In the seventh century of the Common Era Mohammed is said to have claimed that the Golden Rule is the "noblest Religion": "Noblest Religion is this—that you should like for others what you like for yourself; and what you feel painful for yourself, hold that as painful for all others too." Again: "No man is a true believer unless he desires for his brother that which he desires for himself."[7]

The Golden Rule is likewise found in some non-literate religions as well: "One going to take a pointed stick to pinch a baby bird should first try it on himself to feel how it hurts."[8]

The eighteenth-century Western philosopher Immanuel Kant came up with a "rational" version of the Golden Rule in his famous "Categorical Imperative," or "Law of Universal Fairness": "Act on maxims which can at the same time have for their object themselves as universal laws of nature. . . . Treat humanity in every case as an end, never as a means only."[9]

It is clear that the core of the world's major Religions, the Golden Rule, "does not attempt the futile and impossible task of abolishing and annihilating egoism. On the contrary, it makes Egoism the *measure* of Altruism. 'Do not foster the *ego* more than the *alter*; care for the *alter as much as* for the *ego*.' To abolish egoism is to abolish altruism also; and *vice versa*."[10]

Authentic egoism and authentic altruism then are not in conflict with each other; the former necessarily moves to the latter, even, as noted, possibly "giving one's life for one's friend." This, however, is the last and highest stage of human

---

[7] Hadith: Muslim, chapter on iman, 71–2; Ibn Madja, Introduction, 9; Al-Darimi, chapter on riqaq; Hambal 3, 1976. The first quotation is cited in Bhagavan Das *The Essential Unity of All Religions* (1934), p. 298.

[8] A Yoruba Proverb (Nigeria), cited in Andrew Wilson, ed., *World Scripture* (New York: Paragon House, 1991), p. 114.

[9] Immanuel Kant, *Critique of Practical Reason*, A 54; and *Groundwork of the Metaphysics of Ethics*, BA 66f.

[10] Das, *Essential Unity*, p. 303.

development. It is the stage of the (w)holy person, the saint, the arahat, the bodhisattva, the sage. Such a stage cannot be the *foundation* of human society. Rather, it must be the *goal* of it. The foundation of human society must be first self-love, which includes moving outward to loving others. Not recognizing this foundation of self-love is the fundamental flaw of those idealistic systems, such as communism, that try to build a society on the *foundation* of altruism. A human and humanizing society should *lead* toward (w)holiness, toward altruism, but it cannot be built on the assumption that its citizens are (w)holy and altruistic to start with. Such an altruism must grow out of an ever developing self-love; it cannot be assumed, and surely it cannot be forced (as has been tried for decades—with disastrous dehumanizing results).

e) *"Excursus": A Contemporary Marxist Understanding*

A popular level version of Marxism has thought of humanity as essentially determined by great social forces, especially economic, in a way that submerges the individual human person and forecasts the inevitable triumph of Marxism through the inexorable development of a classless society which will have gone through the phases of the dictatorship of the proletariat, socialism and, finally, communism, as described above. Such a crass understanding, however, is not the way a careful Marxist understanding of what it means to be human is presented by "non-orthodox" Marxist thinkers. In the 1960s philosopher and French Communist Party Politibureau member Roger Garaudy stressed that Marxism is not static or pre-determined, but dynamic, relational, and unendingly so:

> The individual for Marx is defined by the whole of his social relations just as the object is defined infinitely, inexhaustibly by its relations with the totality of other objects. The reality with which the physicist has to deal is already, as Lenin wrote, inexhaustible. How much more inexhaustible is the human reality which with life, conscience, society has crossed so many other thresholds of complexity![11]

---

[11] Garaudy, *Anathema*, p. 54.

Such a "relational" understanding of human nature has become more and more widespread in twentieth-century philosophical thinking, and has also become increasingly prominent among Christian thinkers. It is also very like the Buddhist notion of "Dependent Co-origination," and hence of *Sunyata*, which will be discussed below.

Garaudy also emphasized the dynamic, non-determined core of reality in his emphasis on the Marxist notion that *praxis* is the fountain of history and truth. He cited Marx as saying that "men make their own history," and went on to ask, "How, in spite of such insistence, has it been possible to ascribe to Marx a supposed 'economic determinism' which is so contrary to the basic spirit of his doctrine?" He answered that, "superficial disciples or excessively hasty or ill-intentioned opponents have frequently mistaken the true originality of Marx's materialism . . . understanding 'scientific' history to mean a history in which the future has already been written. This is a distortion of the very spirit of Marxism which is essentially *a methodology of historical initiative*."[12] Garaudy secured the validity of his interpretation by a citation of Engels:

> Marx and I are ourselves partly to blame for the fact that younger writers sometimes lay more stress on the economic side than is due to it. We had to emphasize this main principle in opposition to our adversaries, who denied it, and we had not always the time, the place or the opportunity to allow the other elements involved in the interaction to come into their rights.[13]

Decades later the Yugoslav Marxist philosopher from the "Praxis" group, Zagorka Golubovic, argued along a similar line, insisting that according to Marx "the uniqueness of being human cannot be expressed by a definition based on a selection of one of the distinctive traits."[14] Rather, "the very fact that

---

[12] Ibid., p. 73.

[13] Ibid., p. 75.

[14] Zagorka Golubovic, "A Marxist Approach to the Concept of Being/Becoming Human," a paper delivered at the Christian-Marxist dialogue,

men persistently create and recreate themselves speaks against a definition of man in terms of a fixed set of traits." For Marx, a key notion was that of praxis, which helps us understand "that human beings do not exist as 'determined objects,' or as 'unambiguously free subjects,' but as the conscious agents who both construct the world by their actions, and are conditioned and limited by the world they themselves have created."

Golubovic developed this notion of humans as conscious agents, rejecting the vulgarized Marxist concept of economic, or other, determinism: "One cannot speak strictly in terms of determinism when human processes are concerned because the many-sided interactions taking place in the sphere of human conduct are not explainable by the categories of causality." Rather, one must go beyond the usual causal categories; "a new kind of *teleological causality* should be applied when trying to understand human activity and man's relation to his world." As a consequence, "Men's developments depend not only on the given conditions and opportunities, but also on the choices and decisions they have to make . . . in their conscious goal-directed actions."[15]

In the end, Golubovic offered her own description of the constitutive elements of being human, with a strong stress on freedom and the "spiritual" dimensions—not what one usually expects from alleged atheistic dialectical materialists:

"Christian and Marxist Views on the Meaning of Being Human," in Granada, Spain, August 23–27, 1988, sponsored by the New Ecumenical Research Association. Other citations below from Professor Golubovic all come from this paper. See also her essay, "Philosophical Basis of Human Rights in Marxism," Leonard Swidler, ed., *Human Rights: Christians Marxists and Others in Dialogue* (New York: Paragon House, 1991), pp. 71–84.

[15] Professor Golubovic calls attention at this point in a footnote to a very important distinction between what Marx himself thought and what most so-called "orthodox" Marxists taught: "Marx was aware of the fact that social laws appear merely as tendencies, unlike natural laws which have a causal structure and determine the effects. This is a very significant distinction which the Orthodox Marxists failed to make, thanks primarily to a greater influence of Engels' 'dialectics of nature.' However, when the necessary distinction is made it becomes possible to speak of man's freedom as an important component of a specific kind of social determinism which involves the 'teleological causality.' "

a) an evolved psychic structure which is unique to man (which may be named as 'spiritual nature,' expressing a network of many-dimensional psychic traits and abilities); b) a new mode of man-environment relationship (taking freedom as a paradigm which explains how man breaks through natural determinism and causal relations and changes the world); and c) self-actualization as an essential expression of individual existence, which links human characteristics and abilities evolved in the course of socio-cultural evolution of man with the process of personalization.

5. *Ultimate Reality*

Because religion (and ideology) are concerned to provide an explanation of the ultimate meaning of life, two key elements in this explanation obviously are the understanding of human nature and the understanding of Ultimate Reality, for only after at least vaguely grasping these can one hope to explain something of the relationship of the two—being careful not to fall into the trap of trying to explain the two elements and their relationship in a rationalistic manner that so many Christian theologians of past centuries fell into when trying to explain the relationship of an omnipotent God and a radically free human will, referred to above.

Having looked at the various major understandings of human nature, it is necessary to now turn to an investigation of the major understandings of Ultimate Reality. Because the conceptions of Ultimate Reality in the three "Western," or Semitic, religions (Judaism, Christianity, Islam) appear so strikingly different from those of the Eastern religions (Hinduism, Buddhism, Confucianism and Taoism) it will be helpful to look at those understandings by comparing the Eastern and Western notions; that will be followed by a comparative look at a Marxist (as a chief representative of an Ideology) understanding of "ultimate reality."

a) *Hindu and Semitic Understandings*

There are in fact some extremely interesting disparities *and* similarities between the Judeo-Christian-Islamic and the Hindu understandings of Ultimate Reality:

First, both traditions distinguish between Ultimate Reality, "God," in self, *in se*, and God as related to, perceived by, others, *ad extra*. God is said to be in-finite, so any perception of God by something other than God, that is, by something finite, is by the very nature of the knowing receptacle bound to be finite. ("Things known are known according to the mode of the knower," as Thomas Aquinas said.) Hence, God, the in-finite, is not known directly. God is not known *in se*, but only as God relates to non-God, that is, *ad extra*.

This distinction was very clear in the Hebraic tradition as between God, *Yahweh*, whose "face no one can see and live," on the one hand, and the Spirit (*Ruach*) of God, who moves over the waters in creation, and Wisdom (*Hokmah*), through whom all things were created, on the other.[16] An interesting aspect of these depictions (including *Shekhinah* and *Torah*) of the divine *ad extra* is that they are feminine, and not only in grammatical gender, but also in general imagery. This is matched to some extent by the Hindu distinction between *Brahman*, analogous to God *in se*, and the feminine *Shakti*. *Shakti*, like the Hebrew *Ruach* and *Hokmah*, is understood as, "the Divine *Sakti* penetrating everything and manifesting God, disclosing him in his immanence and being present in all his manifestations—this Spirit of God. . . .[17]

In the Christian tradition the feminine figure of Wisdom, *Hokmah*, was in many instances assimilated in its traits into the Christ figure. *Christos* is simply the Greek form of the Hebrew *Meshiach*, the Anointed One, but in Christian tradition it quickly took on the much more far-reaching characteristics of *Hokmah*. This is seen perhaps most strikingly in the Prologue of John's Gospel (John 1:1–4) where the talk is about the Word,

---

[16] In the early Rabbinic period (around the beginning of the Common Era) a third term was also employed to denote God vis-à-vis humanity, God's presence (*Shekhinah*). Wisdom was further identified with another extremely important expression of the divine vis-à-vis humanity, namely, *Torah* (see Ben Sira 24:1–3); the Rabbis made the identification even closer (see *Genesis Rabbah* 1; 8[6a]).

[17] Raimundo Panikkar, *The Unknown Christ in Hinduism*, rev. ed. (Maryknoll, NY: Orbis, 1981), p. 9.

the *Logos*. However, it must be borne in mind that the Jewish Scriptures had already identified God's Word (*Dabar*) with Wisdom (cf. Psalm 119, Ben Sira 24:1–3, 9, 23, also Wisdom 9:1–2), and many Christian Scripture scholars today suggest that in this Prologue *Logos* was simply substituted for *Hokmah/Sophia* in a previously existing hymn to Wisdom.[18] Thus in the Christian tradition *Christos*, *Logos*, are very like the Hebraic figure *Hokmah*, that is, the creative aspect of God, God *ad extra*, and both are like the Hindu *Shakti*, and even more prominently (as will be discussed below) the masculine Lord, *Ishvara*.

Ultimate Reality is not only variously named, but also variously conceived, both West and East. Although the proper Hebraic name for Ultimate Reality, Yahweh (which was long understood to mean, "I am who am," as the Latin Vulgate translates it, but now is usually thought to be more accurately understood as something like the more dynamic, "I will be who I will be"), does seem largely to describe divinity *in se*, the Bible and most subsequent Jewish and Christian writings speak almost exclusively of God *ad extra*. Not so in Hinduism.

The preferred term there for Ultimate Reality is *Brahman* (occasionally referred to as *Atman*, written with a capital "A"). *Brahman* is not exactly divinity *in se*, but at times is understood in a way close to that concept. In that case it is *Brahman* without attributes, *Nirguna Brahman*, as opposed to *Brahman* with attributes, *Saguna Brahman* (this latter being largely identified with the Lord, *Ishvara*). In any case, *Brahman* usually is not thought of as personal, but rather like the "Ground of Being" —"Pure Potency," in Aristotelian terms (quite the opposite of God in the West, who would be thought of rather as "Pure Actuality"). This contrasts with the Judeo-Christian-Islamic understanding of divinity as personal. Hence the Greek term *Theos* (related to the Latin *Deus*, both of which are rendered in English as "God"), including as it does the notion of *personal* divinity, leads to the concept of "theism" as affirming a per-

---

[18] Gerhard Kittel, ed., *Theological Dictionary of the New Testament*, vol. 4 (Grand Rapids, MI: Eerdmans, 1968), pp. 133 ff.

sonal God. In brief, it can be said then that the notion of "God" is personal, theistic, whereas the notion of *Brahman* usually is non-personal, non-theistic.

A related teaching in Hinduism is that at the absolute inner foundation of the human person is the authentic self, or *atman*, and this individual self was seen by the Shankara Advaita (non-dualistic) Hindu tradition to be identified with *Brahman* (sometimes this is expressed: *atman* is *Atman*). Since *Brahman* is the innermost "breath" of everything (as was seen, *atman* fundamentally means "breath"), it is best understood in terms of immanence, the "within" of things—and God in terms of transcendence, the "beyond" all things. The former stresses unity and the latter otherness.

> Indian speculation for the most part is inclined to search for identity; Semitic speculation, on the other hand, characteristically emphasizes the uniqueness of each being and differences between beings. The first kind of mind, typically Indian, probes the depths of being to find the truth; the second kind of mind is directed upwards, looking for the truth in the most sublime heights . . . the conception of Brahman scarcely coincides at all with the conception of God; the two conceptions are almost as opposed as pure potentiality to pure actuality.[19]

However, neither religious tradition was content with affirming its "traditional" conception of Ultimate Reality. The West did try to speak of God *in se*, as, for example, in the Jewish Kabbalah's term *En Sof* (Infinite), from which come Ten Lights, the last of which is the *Shekhinah*, i.e., the manifestation of God to humanity. Of course in Christianity there is the development of the doctrine of the Trinity, which is an attempt to describe God *in se*. The Christian mystic theologian Meister Eckhart in the 13/14th centuries distinguished between the Godhead, which he called *Deitas* (God *in se*) and God, which he called *Deus* (God *ad extra*). In modern times Paul Tillich spoke of "the

---

[19] Panikkar, *Unknown Christ*, p. 140.

God above the God of theism."[20] Alfred North Whitehead and subsequent process theologians have distinguished between the primordial nature of God (*in se*) and the consequent nature of God (*ad extra*). It should be added that the Muslim Sufi term *Al Haqq* as the underlying "abyss" below the personal *Allah*, and the Taoist *Tao Te Ching*'s comment that "the Tao that can be expressed is not the eternal Tao,"[21] are both references to similar distinctions in other major religious traditions.

Although this stress on God *in se*, on divinity in itself, has been relatively less in the Judeo-Christian-Islamic traditions than in the Hindu, every major religious tradition eventually must deal with, reflect, both dimensions: Ultimate Reality *in se* and *ad extra*. How it is done is a question of emphasis.

Though the emphasis in Hinduism has been on Ultimate Reality *in se*, on *Nirguna Brahman*, the notion of God as perceived by humanity, God for us, *ad nos*, did develop and took a form that has some extraordinary parallels to the Jewish, and even more, the Christian tradition. In Hinduism, *Brahman* acting *ad extra* is referred to as Lord, as *Ishvara*:

> Brahman is absolutely transcendent and in a sense beyond being and non-being. It is pure silence and utter nothingness, truly ab-solute, i.e., unrelated. It can thus perform no external function, and it is for this that the figure of Isvara appears. . . . In other words Brahman is devoid of relations, and it is precisely Isvara who provides for them. . . . He is properly speaking, the re-velation of Brahman, the first issue, so to speak, of the unfathomable womb of Brahman. Isvara is God. Brahman cannot be a person, for if it were it would have to relate to others (things or persons), which would compromise its absoluteness. Isvara is the personal aspect of Brahman. . . . Brahman *as such* cannot be creator of the World, again because of its absolute transcendence. Isvara, therefore, is that "aspect" of Brahman responsible for the creation of the World. . . . Brahman is so

---

[20] Paul Tillich, *The Courage to Be* (New Haven: Yale University Press, 1952), p. 190.

[21] Cited in John Hick, *God Has Many Names* (Philadelphia: Westminster Press, 1982), p. 92.

> immutable and unmanifest, beyond every capacity for action, that Isvara has to take over its functions in relation to the universe and to souls.[22]

Despite the differences, the similarities of *Ishvara* to *Ruach*, *Hokmah*, and *Shekhina* in the Hebraic/Jewish tradition and the Spirit, *Logos* and *Christos* in the Christian are striking. Important differences are there also, to be sure: *Hokmah* in the Hebraic tradition is not associated with an historical person, whereas *Christos* is associated with Yeshua of Nazareth; there are "incarnations," "*Avatars*" of *Ishvara* (Vishnu) in Hinduism, e.g., Rama and Krishna, but these are not true historical figures. However, according to the *Bhagavata Purana*, another *Avatar* is Buddha, who was an historical figure.

b) *Buddhist and Semitic Understandings*

The fundamental difference in approach to the basic question of the meaning of life between the Rabbis, Yeshua (as Jesus was called in his native Semitic tongue) and the Muslim Ulama on the one hand and Gautama on the other, and consequently between Judaism-Christianity-Islam and Buddhism, can be summed up in one word: God. In the theistic tradition God is understood in a most positive sense, whereas in Buddhism some of the basic terms—e.g., *Nirvana*, *Sunyata* or emptiness—are either understood in a totally negative manner, or rather, are misunderstood thus by many. Since, however, there has been a growing tendency among both Buddhist and Western scholars either to claim that Gautama's original meaning was ultimately positive, and therefore to give a positive meaning to terms like *Sunyata*—in any case, to make that latter move—the question arises as to whether even in this bedrock difference there might not be the common ground for a fruitful dialogue. The Catholic theologian Hans Küng thus writes:

---

[22] Panikkar, *Unknown Christ*, pp. 152f.

> It has already been indicated how the concept of emptiness in Mahayana has increasingly turned into something positive. . . . For on the highest level of mystical experience the human person recognizes that "emptiness"—beyond all concepts and words—is the expression of the deepest reality, of the Absolute, of that which Christian theology calls "God" . . . as an expression of the "*ineffabilitas*" of the Godhead. . . . Nirvana is understood positively as a happy final goal of unshakable calm, of definitive peace and inexpressible blessedness (instead of *dukkha*, *sukkha* [happiness]) . . . the presentation of *nirvana* then is very like the Christian presentation of "eternal life,"[23]

which for Christians starts not after death, but "now," as also in the teaching of Gautama. Küng then asks the following pointed question: "Would the conclusion be disallowed that that which Christians call 'God' is likewise present under very different names in Buddhism insofar as it does not in principle completely disallow all positive statements? . . . Against the background of what has been developed here, I would like to attempt the answer in a single sentence," which Küng then capsulates as follows:

> If God truly is the Absolute, then he is *all these in one*:
> Nirvana, insofar as he is the goal of the path of liberation;
> Dharma, insofar as he is described as the law of the cosmos and humanity;
> Emptiness, insofar as he constantly escapes all affirmative specifications;
> Primordial Buddha, insofar as he is the origin of all that is.
> Could one not, after all the explanations of emptiness, nirvana and dharmakaya in comparison with the Christian understanding of the Absolute, despite all the divergences, also speak of *convergence between Christianity and Buddhism*?

---

[23] Hans Küng et al., *Christentum und Weltreligionen* (Munich: Piper Verlag, 1984), pp. 492, 491.

Küng then points to the writings of the Japanese Mahayana Kyoto school and the Theravada Thai monk Buddhadasa for contemporary Buddhist substantiation of his position.[24]

It is not only Christian or Western thinkers who have been concerned with trying to express the understanding of Ultimate Reality in ways that will take into account both the various theistic affirmations and the non-theistic affirmation of much of Buddhism. For example, the Zen Buddhist of the Kyoto school, Masao Abe, most recently attempted to build such a bridge between the theistic notion of "God" and Buddhist "Emptiness," "*Sunyata*."[25] To do so he makes use of the Mahayana doctrine of the threefold body, the *Trikaya*, of the Buddha, that is, of Ultimate Reality. In this "trinitarian" doctrine the three bodies are named, first, the manifestation body, *Nirmana-kaya*, second, the heavenly body, *Sambhoga-kaya*, and third, *Dharma-kaya*, in ascending order, as it were. The *Nirmana-kaya* is like the various human manifestations of Ultimate Reality, e.g., Moses, Yeshua, Buddha, Mohammed. The *Sambhoga-kaya* is like the several personal Gods affirmed by the various traditions, e.g., Yahweh, the Holy Trinity, Allah, Ishvara, Amida (of Pure Land Buddhism), who have various virtues, characteristics, names, etc. At the highest point is Ultimate Reality itself, *Dharma-kaya*, which Abe describes as "Formless Emptiness or Boundless Openness."

In many ways this suggestion is reminiscent of the earlier discussion comparing the Semitic and Hindu notions of the Ultimate. On the Hindu side there was the distinction made between *Brahman* without attributes (*Nirguna Brahman*) and *Brahman* with attributes (*Saguna Brahman*, later identified with *Ishvara*), and on the Semitic side the various expressions of the distinction between God *in se* and *ad extra*. It seems that the Semitic, Hindu and Buddhist notions of Ultimate Reality are similar in that they all affirm that the Ultimate is bound-less,

---

[24] Ibid., pp. 551f.

[25] Masao Abe, "A Dynamic Unity in Religious Pluralism: A Proposal from the Buddhist Point of View," John Hick and Hasan Askari, eds., *The Experience of Religious Diversity* (Hants, England: Gower, 1985), pp. 163–190.

in-finite, un-utterable in itself, and that various aspects of it are encountered, perceived by humans. John Hick, in commenting favorably on Abe's suggestion, likens this distinction to that of Kant's distinction between the *noumenon*, the thing in itself, which we do not perceive, and the *phenomena*, which we do.[26]

It is not difficult for thinkers of the Semitic religious traditions and the theistic strand of the Hindu traditions to accept a *theologia negativa*, an apophatic theology, that acknowledges that the grandest proclamations about God are like whispers in the face of the Infinite Hurricane. It is true that the theistic traditions would tend to speak of God more in terms of Pure Act, *Pleroma*, Fullness, rather than Pure Potency, *Sunyata*, Emptiness. However, there might not be the contradiction involved here which appears on the surface, for just as the theistic notion of God as Pure Being is conceived as the very opposite of *Stasis*, namely, as *Dynamis*, so also the non-theist notion of the Ultimate, namely, Nothingness, *das Nichts* (an alternative term of Meister Eckhart's for *Deitas*), Emptiness, *Sunyata*, is also thought of not in static but dynamic terms:

> This Emptiness is not a static state of emptiness, but rather a dynamic activity constantly emptying everything including itself. It is formless formless-ness, takes various forms deeply by negating its own formlessness. This is the reason that "Formless Emptiness" or "Boundless Openness" is here regarded as the ultimate ground which dynamically reveals itself both in terms of personal "Gods" and in terms of "Lords" that are historical religious figures.[27]

Where a more serious difficulty does come in, however, is that the theist tradition is reluctant to give up the affirmation that Ultimate Reality is ultimately personal, and accept that it is "Formless Emptiness" in the sense that negates, or even "goes beyond," the personal in a way that obviates it. The Hindu Santosh Sengupta probably speaks for the theistic tradition in general when he writes: "In the upanishadic view there is no

---

[26] John Hick, "Religious Diversity as Challenge and Promise," ibid., p. 19.

[27] Abe, "Dynamic Unity," p. 184.

negation of the personality of the ultimate. There is no need for the transcendence of personality, for the personality, which the ultimate is, is free from the limitations of human personality."[28]

Perhaps a resolution of the apparent contradiction lies in an analysis of how the human mind and language works. When theists state that the Ultimate is personal they mean to affirm something positive about it. But by the very fact of making an affirmation, the theist necessarily asserts certain limitations, even when s/he immediately rushes in with a "not this, not that," *neti, neti*, disclaimer, asserting that all limitations are automatically to be rejected.

For example, when asserting the positive characteristic of personality the theist will necessarily, if not reject, at least temporarily ignore, the possible characteristics of the Ultimate as Energy, Force, etc. The theist might then hurry to assert: Of course, all the positive characteristics of Energy, Force, etc., are also to be attributed to God. But this task goes on endlessly, or as Abe might say, with "Boundless Openness." This the theist would gladly grant, but would want to add that this "Boundless Openness," far from eliminating or negating the positive affirmations of Personality, Energy, etc., in fact gives them a Boundless Depth, Dynamism, Openness—with which perhaps Masao Abe and much of Buddhism might also agree, and perhaps Taoism as well with its notion of "Dynamic Vacuity," *Kung Ling*.[29]

Exactly what is understood by *Sunyata*, Emptiness, warrants a little more probing. It can be said that Emptiness is another name for the Buddhist doctrine of *Pratitya samutpada*, Dependent Origination, which in short means that nothing exists as a self-subsisting isolated thing. Rather, everything is ultimately a net of relationships, and consequently is always in flux, is "becoming." This of course is not a new thought to the

---

[28] Santosh Chandra Sengupta, "The Misunderstanding of Hinduism," John Hick, ed., *Truth and Dialogue in World Religions: Conflicting Truth Claims* (Philadelphia: Westminster, 1974), p. 97.

[29] See Tang Yi, "Taoism as a Living Philosophy," *Journal of Chinese Philosophy*, 12:4 (December 1985), p. 408.

West; it was expounded by the ancient Greek Heraclitus (536–470 B.C.E.), a near-contemporary of Gautama's (563–483 B.C.E.).

However, this relational understanding has received greater prominence in the West in recent times. It is largely from the second century C.E. Nagarjuna, the second patriarch of Mahayana Buddhism, that the doctrine of *Sunyata* comes. He clearly denied that there are any self-subsisting substances, but insisted that whatever "is" at any moment of space-time consists of conditions or relationships, and these too are dependently co-originated: "The 'originating dependently' we call 'emptiness.' " "Emptiness *is* dependent co-origination."[30]

It should also be noted that how one describes Ultimate Reality is, among other things, dependent upon one's culture. What is thought to be of greatest value in a culture will be attributed to Ultimate Reality; the fact that Ultimate Reality is so described will, of course, in turn dialectically reinforce that value in the culture.

For example, when females were thought to be the sole source of life, and hence, power, divinities were described in female terms—which in fact is how divinities first turn up in human cultures, as we know from archeological excavations at the most primitive layers. However, when it was discovered that males also played a role in producing new life, male divinities slowly began to appear and develop. As cultures became patriarchal—and practically all cultures did by the time humankind arrived at the historical period of development (around 3000 B.C.E., when writing was first invented in Sumer)—it became less and less acceptable to refer to the divinity as female. Hence, for example, God became almost exclusively a male, father God in the Semitic traditions; it would have been denigrating and blasphemous to refer to God in female terms, because woman was of lesser value in the culture.

So it was also for a long time in Western culture concerning

---

[30] Nagarjuna cited in Paul O. Ingram, "Buddhist and Christian Paradigms of Selfhood," typescript paper delivered at January 3–11, 1984 conference at Honolulu on "Paradigm Shift in Buddhism and Christianity: Cultural Systems and the Self."

the notions of "being," "substance," "stability," and the like. These were high values in the culture, so naturally they were attributed to the Ultimate Reality. But now in the West immutability, substance, *status quo*, etc., are increasingly less valued as compared with change, relationality, evolution. Hence, earlier in the West where it would have been difficult to speak of Ultimate Reality as being in constant change, in complete relationship, etc., for it would have seemed to be saying that the Ultimate Reality was less than ultimate—with the recent cultural shift, to speak thus seems to be more and more appropriate. Consequently, a Methodist theologian, for example, could publish an article entitled, "Can God Be Change Itself?" and conclude in the affirmative, insisting that this was more in keeping with the original genius of the Hebrew God, whose very name, Yahweh, as noted above, means "I will be who I will be"—always changing.[31]

But what about the apparently opposite trend in the modern Judeo-Christian tradition, namely, the emphasis not on the Emptiness of Ultimate Reality, of God, but on God's passion, commitment, involvement, in history, and particularly on the side of the oppressed—the talk of God as the "God of the Oppressed"? This tradition grew out of the line of the Hebrew prophets, continued in Judeo-Christian history, and was expanded in the nineteenth century as the Western awareness of the influence in human life of social structures grew, and that religion had to be concerned about changing them for the better if the individuals were to be changed for the better. This led in the last hundred years, e.g., to the Jewish passion for social justice, the Jüdischer Bund, Christian Socialism, the Social Gospel, and the several contemporary "liberation" theologies. One Christian answer has been that,

> Liberation theologies can themselves learn from Buddhism that the "God of the Oppressed" to whom they point is also a "God who is empty." . . . in a Buddhist sense, referring to that absence of self-subsistence and, hence, that radi-

---

[31] Jung Young-Lee, "Can God Be Change Itself?" *Journal of Ecumenical Studies*, 10:4 (Fall 1973), pp. 752–70.

> cal relationality of which all beings are exemplifications. To say that God is "empty" is to say that God, too, is relational. It is to affirm (1) that the efficacy of God's action in the world depends partly on worldly response, and (2) that the world's sufferings are God's own.[32]

c) *Confucian and Semitic Understandings*

There of course was religion in China before Confucius (c. 552–479 B.C.E.) and the legendary founder of Taoism, Laotzu (perhaps fifth century B.C.E.), but they gave it a classical, highly developed form, or rather, forms, for Confucianism and Taoism, though they influenced each other considerably, are very different from each other.

Julia Ching notes that "From his own account of spiritual evolution, it might also be inferred that Confucius was a religious man, a believer in Heaven as personal God, who sought to understand and follow Heaven's Will."[33] Her own understanding of religion, she says, includes a consciousness of a dimension of transcendence that "I perceive as present in Confucianism from the very beginning, even though this has not always referred to a belief in a personal deity. . . . The very insistence upon the priority of the 'way of Heaven,' and the quest itself for the discovery and fulfillment of such within the way of man, point to a movement toward self-transcendence," and consequently Confucianism "remains religious at its core, on account of its spiritual teachings of sagehood or self-transcendence."[34]

Closely connected to this question is the understanding and even the name of the transcendent in Confucianism. Careful research has shown that already in the Shang period (1766–1123 B.C.E.) the term *Shang-Ti* (Lord on High) or *Ti* (Lord) was used to refer to the highest of the gods and eventually to a transcendent being, perhaps even a creator god. In the Chou

---

[32] Jay McDaniel, "The God of the Oppressed and the God Who Is Empty," *Journal of Ecumenical Studies*, 23:3 (Fall 1985), p. 687.

[33] Hans Küng and Julia Ching, *Christentum und chinesche Religion* (Munich: Piper Verlag, 1988), p. 95.

[34] Ibid., p. 116.

period (1122–249 B.C.E.) the term most often used for God was *T'ien* (Heaven), symbolized by a large human head. After the Chou conquered the Shang both *Ti* and *T'ien* were used to refer to God, understood as a personal God.

The nineteenth-century English Protestant missionary and translator of many of the Chinese religious classics, James Legge, found in his research the name for the highest God, *Shang-Ti*. "There was, then, before Confucius and many of the sage kings, a monotheistic religion: '*the* Confucian religion' "[35] Of course even earlier, in the sixteenth century, the great Catholic scholar, scientist and missionary to China, Matteo Ricci, learned much the same about Chinese, and especially Confucian, religion as Legge later did, and wrote accordingly.

Though many traditions see the transcendent and the immanent as opposites, the contemporary Confucian Mou Tsung-san "sees the Confucian as joining the ethical and religious dimensions in an effective unity of lived experience. . . . There is no ultimate separation of the subjective and objective, the inner and outer, the immanent and the transcendent."[36]

Already in the writings of Mencius (371–289 B.C.E.) we find the tendency to speak less in terms of a personal God, or in terms of the Transcendent as *ganz anders*, completely other, but more in terms of the Transcendent, Heaven, being reflected in the human heart: Who knows his/her own heart and nature also knows Heaven.[37] Hence, the Transcendent, instead of being "out there," more and more was found within, immanent. Such an understanding of course is very congenial to a very important strand in the Judeo-Christian tradition, starting already with the creation story where it is said that humanity is made in God's image.

It is in this relationship between the Transcendent and the

---

[35] Ibid., p. 42.

[36] Mou Tsung-san, *Chung-kuo che-hsüeh t'e-chi* [The Uniqueness of Chinese Philosophy] (Taipei: Student Book Co., 1974), as cited by John Berthrong, "Adjustments: Dual Transcendence and Fiduciary Community," a paper delivered at the Hong Kong International Christian-Confucian Conference, June 8–15, 1988.

[37] *Book of Mencius*, 7a, 1.

Immanent, between Heaven and Humanity, that Confucianism's special characteristic comes to the fore. The core of Confucianism is humanism, but a humanism which, as the contemporary Confucian Tu Wei-ming put it, includes "*a faithful dialogical response to the transcendent.*" He goes on to say that "the mutuality of Heaven and man (in the gender neutral sense of humanity) makes it possible to perceive the transcendent as immanent." In other words, "the Confucians advocate a humanism which neither denies nor slights the transcendent. . . . Humanity is Heaven's form of self-disclcsure, self-expression, and self-realization."[38] Already in 1958 a number of Chinese scholars in Taiwan issued "A Manifesto for the Reappraisal of Sinology and Reconstruction of Chinese Culture" in which "the harmony of the 'way of Heaven' (*T'ien-tao*) and the 'way of man (*Ren-tao*) is extolled by those who signed it as the central legacy of Confucianism."[39]

Again, in this conceptualization there are certain parallels to a Christian theology of the *Imago Dei*, or of an incarnational theology; perhaps most of all it is like Hegel's notion of *Welt Geist*—this latter parallel especially offers to Western, including Christian, thinkers many possibilities, as well as problems. But of course Hegel's thought, and that of all modern historical, dynamic, processive, immanentist thought stands in severe tension with much of traditional Christian philosophy and theology because, as noted previously, the older tradition gave Being, Stasis, Non-change the pride of place, whereas much of contemporary thought holds up Becoming, the Dynamic, Change as the highest value, seeing the static as the mode of death.

Nevertheless, as I have argued earlier in these pages, the stress on the dynamic is clearly the mode of thought of more and more critical-thinking persons, including Christian theologians—witness Vatican II and subsequent Catholic and Protes-

---

[38] Tu Wei-ming, "On Confucian Religiousness," paper delivered at June 8–15, 1988 Hong Kong international Confucian-Christian conference.

[39] Carsun Chang, *The Development of Neo-Confucian Thought*, vol. 2, Appendix (New York, 1963) as cited in Küng and Ching, *Christentum und chinesche Religion*, pp. 123f.

tant theology, despite various inevitable temporary backlash movements. Hence, here is a very promising contemporary basis for Christian, and other, dialogue with Confucianism: Because "being religious, in the Confucian perspective . . . means being engaged in the *process* of learning to be fully human,"[40] and learning to become "human is the real informing characteristic of all authentic Confucian religious sentiment. This *process* of 'humanization' has no limits and is therefore called a transcendent reference . . . the *process* is unending in its scope and completely moral in its intention, while transcendent in ultimate reference."[41]

If for Confucianism, and Christianity, becoming human is an unending process which aims at an ever receding horizon of Heaven, God, the Transcendent ("Our inborn ability to respond to the bidding of Heaven impels us to extend our human horizon continuously so that the immanent in our nature assumes a transcendent dimension"[42]), Confucians make clear that it is a process that is engaged in by self-transcendence, self-effort: "The Confucian faith in the perfectibility of human nature through self-effort is, strictly speaking, a faith in self-transcendence."[43] Mou Tsung-san speaks in similar terms, stressing the centrality of creativity in being human: "For him the heart of being human is creative reason, the capacity to transform self and relate in a meaningful and humane way to others. The essence of being human is hence the creation of new values."[44]

d) *Taoist and Semitic Understandings*

Tao of course means "Way," though it also has the meaning of "Word" or "Saying." It implies that humans are to follow the "Way," but it is quite the opposite of the Jewish and Muslim analogues, *Halacha* and *Shar'ia*. These latter two, as seen above, came to have a specialized meaning of the legal deci-

---

[40] Tu Wei-ming, "On Confucian Religiousness," p. 2.
[41] Berthrong, "Adjustments," p. 11.
[42] Tu Wei-ming, "On Confucian Religiousness," p. 8.
[43] Ibid.
[44] Berthrong, "Adjustments," p. 46.

sions of the proper Way to live. For Taoism, following the Tao essentially means "doing nothing" (*wu wei*) in the sense of being unattached to any particular thing, and thereby living in harmony with Ultimate Reality, which is also named Tao.

Tao as Ultimate Reality, however, is the all-embracing first and last principle, indefinable, unutterable, and indescribable, the "Ground of all worlds before all worlds," which existed even before heaven and earth. It is the mother of everything; and it calls all things into being, without action, in stillness. It is the "power" (*Te*) of Tao that is working in all creation, all unfolding, and all preservation of the world. It is the *Te* of Tao in all appearances that makes them what they are; but the Tao with its power is nowhere tangible or available. Tao is a "not-being" in the sense of "not-being-thus": it is "empty," without any characteristics that are perceptible to the senses. If, however, everything that exists is the Tao, then it would seem that the Tao is identical with *Being*, that is, not "Being" understood in a static Greek sense, but rather in the dynamic modern sense —"Being" understood as "Being in Becoming."

However, if Tao can be understood as "Being," as "Being in Becoming," then is it not ultimately identical with God? Of course, this can not be meant in a primitive anthropomorphic or in an ontological, pantheistic sense, but in the differentiated way of the Western philosophical/theological tradition from Augustine through Thomas to Nicholas of Cusa: as "Being Itself" (*Ipsum Esse Subsistens*) to which the being of all contingently existing beings refers.

Hans Küng asks, "If *nothingness* is the *veil of being* through which being reveals itself, then could the *being* in which humanity participates not also be understood as the *veil of God*?" His response is that, "the being of what exists in becoming covers over the 'Being Itself' that can rightly be called God." Conversely, "the Tao can be identified with the original and final reality."[45] "It can be identified with ultimate transcen-

---

[45] Hans Küng and Julia Ching, *Christianity and Chinese Religions* (New York: Doubleday, 1989), p. 174. I am particularly grateful to Hans Küng in this section for insight into Taoism.

dent reality ([Henri] Maspero)."[46] Hence, there is a possible parallel in structure in the concepts of Tao, Being and God which could be of great importance to the understanding of Ultimate Reality that would bridge cultures and religions.

One more important point needs to be looked at here. During the Han dynasty (206 B.C.E.–220 C.E.) *yin-yang* thinking began to be absorbed into both Confucianism and Taoism. Although a superficial reading of the Taoist material might give one the impression that the claim is made that Ultimate Reality is somehow a combination of opposites, *yin* and *yang*, dark and light, good and evil, such a reading would indeed be superficial, for in the *Tao-te ching* itself the Tao is *prior* to heaven and earth, that is, before duality.

Küng notes: "Indeed, the Tao is before the one and the two, is the origin of the world before all worlds, and is thus the origin of the polarity, not the polarity itself," and adds: "No, an ultimate reality that is both double-sided and contradictory is part of neither the great Chinese nor the great Western tradition. Only penultimate reality is double-sided and contradictory."[47]

Thus, one can say that Tao is unchanging "Being" behind all reality—like the early Chinese understanding of the "Lord-on-High," *Shang-ti* (God *in se*), but it later also takes over the active aspect of "Heaven," *T'ien* (God *ad extra, ad nos*) for it is then also understood as a "divine" pattern for humans to follow (not unlike the Jewish *Torah*).

In the end, Christians can on the basis of their tradition of mystical and negative theologies appreciate completely why Taoists refuse all definitions of the Tao, whether positive or negative. Even that giant of Christian speculative theology, Thomas Aquinas, insists that God's proper essence remains inaccessible to human reason and concurs with the mystic Pseudo-Dionysius when he writes: "Wherefore man reaches the highest point of his knowledge about God when he knows

---

[46] G. H. Dunstheimer, *Histoire des religions*, ed. by H. C. Puech (Paris: 1976), vol. 3, p. 389.

[47] Küng and Ching, *Christianity and Chinese Religions*, p. 177.

that he knows him not, inasmuch as he knows that which is God transcends whatever he conceives of him."[48]

e) *Marxist and Christian Understandings*

At first blush one might assume that Marxists would have no notion of ultimate reality, but if the term is not filled ahead of time with theistic content, the matter is not so simple. For example, Roger Garaudy, as representative of Marxist thinkers who have in the past several decades been in serious dialogue with Christians,[49] sees in the positive attitude toward matter, evolution, the immanent force within matter rising unendingly up to the level of consciousness and beyond, as expressed preeminently in the thought and writings of the Jesuit scientist-theologian Pierre Teilhard de Chardin, a Copernican turn in Christian thought that enables Marxists not only to join with Christians in "building the earth," as Teilhard put it, but also to learn something from them in their efforts to relate the immanent and transcendent in the universe. As Garaudy cited Teilhard: "The synthesis of the [Christian] God of the Above and the [Marxist] God of the Ahead: this is the only God whom we shall in the future be able to adore in spirit and in truth."[50]

This Teilhardian idea is also much like the notion of Karl Rahner's that the Ultimate of humankind is the Absolute Future, the ever receding, ever beckoning Horizon within which humankind lives and moves forward. Garaudy, as noted above, understood Marxism to see the future of humankind similarly: "Yes, man will always be capable of an always greater future."

Writing in 1965, Garaudy argued that for a quarter of a century there had been an "intellectual hardening of the arteries within Marxism," but then there was a "vigorous reappearance of the problems of subjectivity, choice and spiritual re-

---

[48] Cited in Thomas Aquinas, *De Potentia*, q. 7, a. 5. English: *On the Power of God* (London, 1934), vol. 3, p. 33.

[49] See, e.g., Leonard Swidler, *After the Absolute. The Dialogical Future of Religious Reflection* (Minneapolis: Fortress Press, 1990), chapter "Dialogue with Ideologies: Marxism," pp. 165–189.

[50] Garaudy, *Anathema*, p. 54. The several following citations from Garaudy are also all taken from this book.

sponsibility." Garaudy insisted that, "this development has occurred because of the inescapable abandonment of old values and the birth-pangs which accompany the creation of new ones," but granted that "to the extent that Marxism has failed to answer these questions adequately, youth has turned elsewhere to seek the answer which it is our job today to seek, though we may not yet fully discover it." He emphasized that in seeking for answers to these critical human questions Marxism, at least in part, could not evade the quest for what it

> owes to Christianity as a religion of the absolute future and as a contributing factor in the exploration of the two essential dimensions of man: subjectivity and transcendence. We cannot, without impoverishing ourselves, forget Christianity's basic contribution: the change in man's attitude toward the world, preparing a place for subjectivity.

Moreover, he claimed that he was not alone in "this realization of the Christian contribution to civilization and culture, and of the revolutionary potential of the faith," which he said had been "operative not only within the French Communist Party since the great step forward in 1937 but also within all . . . those countries where progressive movements were taking shape within the Catholic Church," meaning especially Italy and Spain.

Garaudy claimed that Marxism has an interest in the questions raised by women and men "about the meaning of their life and their death, about the problem of their origin and their end, about the demands of their thought and their heart," and granted that there is much that "Marxists must assimilate from the rich Christian heritage." However, he went on to claim that although the greatness of religion is displayed by its awareness and concern for these fundamental human questions, its weakness is in its fixing of its once-given answers as always-given answers, despite humanity's advances in thought and ways of understanding. Marxism and Christianity, he stated, both live under the same exigencies, but they differ in their answers:

He began by saying that, "If we reject the very name of God, it is because the name implies a presence, a reality, whereas it is only an exigency which we live, a never-satisfied exigency of totality and absoluteness, of omnipotence as to nature and of perfect loving reciprocity of consciousness." But then he added that, "We can live this exigency, and we can act it out, but we cannot conceive it, name it or expect it. Even less can we hypostatize it under the name of transcendence. Regarding this totality, this absolute, I can say everything except: It is. For what it is is always deferred, and always growing."

Garaudy then wanted to stake out a claim for Marxism of both a doctrine of subjectivity and of transcendence, an unendingly self-transcending future for humanity: "I think that Marxist atheism deprives man only of the illusion of certainty, and that the Marxist dialectic, when lived in its fullness, is ultimately richer in the infinite and more demanding still than the Christian transcendence." But, "it is undoubtedly such only because it bears within itself the extraordinary Christian heritage, which it must investigate still more," and in the end it "owes it to itself in philosophy to work out a more profound theory of subjectivity, one which is not subjectivist, and a more profound theory of transcendence, one which is not alienated."

Most Christian theologians will today admit that the old arguments for the existence of God do not have the rational force of a demonstration that they were once thought to have had. Many will with Hans Küng claim that in the end it is reasonable to affirm the existence of God, not ineluctably so, but in fundamental trust, although in the very affirmation one is confirmed in the reasonableness of one's affirmation.[51] The transcendental theologians and philosophers, like Karl Rahner and Joseph Marechal, however, have argued that the very presence of the open-ended thirst for knowledge, for being, found in the inner nature of humankind, demands that there be an open-ended Source and Goal of that spiritual drive. Garaudy took that idea up when he said, "my thirst does not prove the existence of the spring." But ultimately doesn't it? Is it conceivable in this world as we know it that there could develop a being which has a need for something, say, water, if there were no

---

[51] Hans Küng, *Does God Exist?* (New York: Doubleday, 1980).

such thing as water? No, it would die aborning. But humankind has not died aborning. Therefore. . . .[52]

In any case, Garaudy took seriously the Teilhardian-Rahnerian notion of God as no-*thing*, as the unendingly, infinite-ly creative, absolute future (again reminding one of Buddhism's "Boundless Openness," *Sunyata*): "In such a perspective God is no longer a being nor even the totality of being, since such a totality does not exist. Being is totally open to the future to be created. Faith is not the possession of an object by cognition." He then added that, "the transcendence of God implies its constant negation since God is constant creation beyond any essence and any existence. A faith which is only assertion would be credulity. Doubt is part and parcel of living faith. The depth of faith in a believer depends upon the force of the atheist he bears in himself and defends against all idolatry."

For his part, of course, Garaudy did not find what theists call a divine presence, but only its absence. Still, he was aware that his affirmation of absence was also not an ineluctable rational affirmation, but likewise a choice of his whole being, and in that sense, a "faith": "We thus reach the highest level of the dialogue, that of the integration in each of us of that which the other bears in himself, as other. I said earlier that the depth of a believer's faith depends upon the strength of the atheism that he bears in himself. I can now add: the depth of an atheist's humanism depends on the strength of the faith he bears in himself."

(More than twenty years later the Hungarian Marxist Pal Horvath made a similar point when is said "that the existence of God cannot be theoretically proved or denied. . . . Whoever sees the essence of Marx's atheism in this is mistaken." He then quoted another Hungarian Marxist, Tamas Nyiri, saying: "Until a communist society without religion has developed, the Marxist theory pretending that religion is essentially a false form of consciousness, cannot be considered as proved. It is just one

---

[52] See Anthony Matteo, "Joseph Marechal and the Transcendental Turn in Catholic Thought," (Ph.D. dissertation, Temple University, 1985).

of several potential theories to be verified or refuted by historical-social practice." After all, Horvath said, "When we turn to the question of whose ultimate hypotheses of a cosmic nature will prove true, I am convinced that an answer can only be expected in a perspective of world history."[53])

Garaudy in the end pleaded—to both sides obviously—for the dialogue to continue and deepen—both the ideological and practical dialogue. He said that it would be one of the tragedies of history "if the dialogue between Christians and Marxists and their cooperation for mutual enrichment and for the common building of the future, the city of man, the total man, were still longer to be spoiled, perhaps even prevented, by the weight of the past." He was not asking for "conversion" of one side to the other, but rather, "we offer a dialogue without prejudice or hindrance. We do not ask anyone to stop being what he is. What we ask is, on the contrary, that he be it more and that he be it better." He then added that, "we hope that those who engage in dialogue with us will demand the same of us."

All this is rather stunning stuff, coming as it did from a Marxist philosopher and French Politbureau member of such prominence and profundity. Garaudy admonished, however: "Let us be clearly aware of the fact that we are still only at the start of a great turning point in the epic of man. The turning point itself will not be reached until we have graduated from the meetings of a few lonely scouts, possibly even suspect in their own communities, to the authentic dialogue of the communities themselves." Then in words that were much too painfully prophetic he continued: "The road is heavily ambushed and . . . we must confess that present political conditions do not make any the easier the requisite clarification of the problems." That was 1965. Then came 1968 Soviet crushing of the "Prague Spring," (against which Garaudy spoke out vigorously) and Garaudy's expulsion from the Communist Party in

---

[53] Pal Horvath, "Changes in the Evaluation of Religion and the Churches in the Last Decade in Hungary and the U.S.A.," paper delivered at the Christian-Marxist dialogue held in the Law School of the University of Budapest, June 20–25, 1988.

1970, and similar retrenchments elsewhere which just about destroyed the dialogue between Christians and Marxists for a number of years.

Eventually the dialogue did revive slowly in the late 1970s and into the 1980s, but then quite suddenly became largely moot with the "Great Transformation" in Eastern Europe in 1989–90, which left very few reputable thinkers overtly espousing Marxist ideology. In China, the one remaining major Marxist stronghold, there do not seem to be any Marxist thinkers, only political ideologues. Still, the serious Marxist thinking by reflective philosophers like Garaudy in the 1960s, Golubovic in the 1980s, and others, offers an approach to the questions of Ultimate Reality by a very important and influential ideology in human history.

6. *Interim Conclusion I*

If these reflections are at all close to the mark in trying to discern the meaning of Religion (and Ideology), then I would like to draw them together in a kind of summary of what Religion means and what its purpose is. The definition of Religion I began with in fact was my conclusion after much study and reflection. Hence, I would simply paraphrase it here, stressing its various elements with the help of the four "C's" and "T" (the "Transcendent"):

Religion is an *explanation* (Creed) of the ultimate meaning of life, and *how to live* (Code and Community-structure) accordingly, which is based on the notion of the *Transcendent* (Cult). Because Religion is an explanation of the *ultimate* meaning of life it provides a code of behavior in the fullest possible sense, including all the psychological, social and cultural dimensions of human life, and is hence a "Way of Life"—for *humans*. The "Way of Life" Religion tries to provide, however, is not just any more or less acceptable way of life, but it is an attempt on the basis of its "explanation" and experience to put forth the best possible "Way of Life."

As has been seen, there are many different ways of describing the best possible "Way of Life" which will lead humans most effectively to the goal of life, which is also variously described according to the various religious "explanations" of the ultimate meaning of life. What they all surely have in common, however, is that they aim at providing *humans* with the best possible way to live so as to attain the goal of their lives. Hence, it can be concluded that all religions aim ultimately at making humans as authentically and wholly human as possible —that is, they aim to provide "salvation," however it is described, for humans, however they are understood.

There is also a variety of ways of understanding Ultimate Reality, with a major distinction between the theist, personal understanding on the one hand, and the non-theist, non-personal on the other. Still, the theistic understandings of Ultimate Reality also make room for non-personal understandings —without forfeiting their personal understanding. Also, some versions of the non-personal understanding, especially in dialogue, also stretch to make room for a "personal" understanding of God, as for example in the writings of the Zen Buddhist Masao Abe, who has been deeply involved in dialogue with Christians. There is promise of a deeper, richer understanding of Ultimate Reality by both theists and non-theists in pursuance of dialogue. The dialogue, temporarily largely in abeyance, between adherents of Religion and of Ideology also gives promise of leading to a further understanding of what it means to be human.

III. RELIGIONS AND IDEOLOGIES—THEIR RELATIONSHIP

1. *The Age of Dialogue*

It is becoming increasingly clear that religions and ideologies can no longer exist in complete opposition to each other. It is less and less possible for adherents of a religion or ideology to insist that they alone possess all the truth about the "ultimate meaning of life and how to live accordingly." To be sure there still are many of a fundamentalist mentality in all religions and ideologies who continue to think this way, but even many fundamentalist types in the world's religions and ideologies are coming to admit the necessity of a dialogue of some sort with other religions and ideologies. The Age of Monologue is passing away and the Age of Dialogue is being ushered in.

There are many reasons for this "changing of the Ages," some of which are quite obvious: The people of the world no longer can live in isolation from each other as they largely did in the past. Not only do an increasing number travel all over the globe, but the whole globe, including persons from all the religions and ideologies of the world, comes into hundreds of millions of living rooms through television. For scores of millions, Asian Buddhist monks, Iranian ayatollahs, Sikh militants, Hindu fundamentalists, black African Anglican archbishops, Haitian Catholic priests-become-president, etc. are no longer strangers. Further, all are growing increasingly interdependent for their livelihoods. What governments do in Japan, Iraq,

Germany, the U.S., etc. affects numberless millions around the world, at times massively and almost instantly.

A much deeper major cause, however, of the transition from the Age of Monologue to the Age of Dialogue is the profound paradigm-shift that has been occurring in the West—and now everywhere—in the past hundred years or so in how we perceive and describe the world.

A paradigm is the model, the cluster of assumptions, on whose basis phenomena are perceived and explained: For example, the geocentric paradigm for explaining the movements of the planets; a shift to another paradigm, as to the heliocentric, will—and did!—have a major impact. Such a paradigm-shift recently, and currently, has been taking place in the Western understanding of truth statements, and this has made dialogue not only possible, but even necessary.

Whereas the notion of truth in the West was largely absolute, static, monologic or exclusive up to the last century, it has subsequently become deabsolutized, dynamic and dialogic—in a word: relational. This "new" view of truth came about in at least six different but closely related ways:

Previous View: In Europe before the nineteenth century *truth*, that is, a *statement about reality*, was conceived in an absolute, static, exclusivistic either-or manner. It was thought that if an assertion was true at one time, it was always true, and not only in the sense of statements about empirical facts but also in the sense of statements about the meaning of things. This is a *classicist* or *absolutist* ("absolute" comes from the Latin "ab-solvere," "to loose from" all limitations or conditions, so "absolute" means complete, unlimited) view of truth.

1) In the nineteenth century scholars came to perceive all statements about the meaning of something as being partially products of their historical circumstances; only by placing truth statements in their historical situations, their historical *Sitz im Leben*, could they be properly understood: A text could be understood only in con-text. Hence, all statements about the meaning of things were seen to be "deabsolutized," that is, "limited," in terms of time. This is an *historical* view of truth.

2) Later it was noted that we ask questions so as to obtain knowledge, truth, according to which we want to live; what questions we ask and how we pose them largely determine the shape of the answers we arrive at, i.e., they condition or deabsolutize our statements about reality—truth. This is a *praxis* or *intentional* view of truth, that is, a statement has to be understood in relationship to the action-oriented intention of the thinker.

3) Early in this century Karl Mannheim developed what he called the sociology of knowledge, which points out that every statement about the truth of the meaning of something is perspectival, for all reality is perceived, and spoken of, from the cultural, class, sexual, and so forth, perspective of the perceiver. My view of, and subsequent statement about, reality will be true if I am careful about accuracy, but it will always be from my perspective, and therefore necessarily limited, partial—deabsolutized. This is a *perspectival* view of truth.

4) Ludwig Wittgenstein and many other thinkers discovered something of the limitations of human language: Every description of reality is necessarily only partial, for although reality can be seen from an almost limitless number of perspectives, human language can express things from only one perspective at once. Moreover, this partialness and limitedness of all language is unavoidably greatly intensified when one attempts to speak of the "Transcendent," which by "definition" "goes-beyond." This is a *language-limited* view of truth.

5) The contemporary discipline of hermeneutics (Greek for "interpretation") stresses that all knowledge is interpreted knowledge. That means that in all knowledge it is "*I*" who come to know something; the object comes into me in a certain way, namely, through the lens that I use to perceive it. It was noted before that Thomas Aquinas said, *Cognita sunt in cognoscente secundum modum cognoscentis*, "Things known are in

the knower according to the mode of the knower."[54] This is an *interpretative* view of truth.

6) Still further, reality can "speak" to me only with the language that I give it. The "answers" that I receive back from reality will always be in the language, the thought categories, of the questions I put to it. If the answers I receive are sometimes confused and unsatisfying, then I probably need to learn to speak a more appropriate language when I put questions to reality. As noted before, if I, for example, ask the question, "How far is yellow?" I will receive a non-sense answer. Or if I ask questions about living things in mechanical categories, I will receive confusing and unsatisfying answers. Thus, many receive confusing and unsatisfying answers to questions about human sexuality when categories that are solely physical and biological are used. Witness the absurdity of the answer that birth control is forbidden by natural law; the question falsely assumes that the nature of humanity is merely physical and biological. This understanding of truth is a *dialogic* understanding, which again "deabsolutizes" truth.

In short, our understanding of truth and reality has been undergoing a radical shift. This new paradigm which is being born understands all statements about reality, especially about the meaning of things, to be 1) historical, 2) praxial or intentional, 3) perspectival, 4) language-limited or partial, 5) interpretive, and 6) dialogic. Said other, our understanding of truth statements has become "deabsolutized"—it has become "relational." That is, all statements about reality are now seen to be *related* to the historical context, praxis intentionality, perspective, etc. of the speaker, and in that sense no longer unlimited or "absolute." Hence, my perception and description of the world can be true, but only in a limited sense, that is, only as seen from my place in the world; however, if I wish to expand

---

[54] Thomas Aquinas, *Summa Theologiae*, II-II, Q. 1, a. 2.

my grasp of reality, I need to learn from others what they know of reality that they can perceive from their place in the world, but which I cannot see from mine. That can happen only through dialogue.

2. *Results of Interreligious, Interideological Dialogue*

What results of the dialogue among religions, and ideologies, can be looked for? In general we can expect not only a proportional cessation of violence—physical, verbal, economic, etc.—but also a burst of creativity. It is obvious that the diminishing of hostility in the world will automatically raise the level of "happiness" in the world. But beyond that, it is also true that the energy—particularly psychic and intellectual energy—otherwise poured into polemics, overt and covert, will then be released for constructive rather than destructive purposes. But will these newly freed forces not be turned to other wasteful or even destructive uses? Possible.

However, the overwhelming likelihood is that they will be focussed on a creative expansion of the individual's authentic self, which very much includes relations with others—other persons, animals, inanimate things, and finally, Ultimate Reality. The reasons for this are several:

a) *Dialogue Partners Serve as Mirrors*

First, in dialogue the partners also serve as mirrors for each other. The same basic human law of becoming more wholly human through mutuality referred to above operates very centrally here in dialogue. Every person entering dialogue will have a certain self-understanding. However, in the dialogue they will not only learn more about the partners which they did not know before, they will also learn how the partners have perceived them.

Even if the first dialogue partners claim that the second have misunderstood them—which to a greater or lesser extent normally happens—the first partners will learn how they de facto have been seen by at least some others—and this "relationship" of being perceived by others is also very much a part of their own reality. Relationships are essential, constitutive elements of each human (of every being, for that matter). Humans live not as atomized "monads" but in groups; as Aristotle noted, humans are gregarious animals (as in the Latin *gregis*, "flock"). Through their dialogue partners humans learn an additional piece of "how they are in the world," as Heidegger might put it.

Since in dialogue people come primarily to learn from the other and then to change accordingly, this learning to know how others perceive them will also tend to have a transformative effect on the first partners. For example, if the first partners understand themselves to be tolerant, but they frequently learn that others perceive them as intolerant, they will perhaps try to change their way of acting so as to communicate what they believe is their authentic self. Or they may be forced, after reflection, to admit to themselves that they in fact were not as tolerant as they thought they were and then either move to change their inner reality and become more tolerant, or change their understanding of tolerance, or perhaps decide they are being as "tolerant" as they believe they, with integrity, ought to be (e.g., they judge they should not be "tolerant" of racism).

b) *Shift from Inward to Outward Looking*

Secondly, entering into serious interreligious, interideological dialogue entails shifting from a kind of inward staring—whose concomitant move is to sally forth to persuade or attack the outsider—to a looking outward. This is a fundamental, radical shift which normally will utterly transform the dialogue partners. The outside religious world is now no longer perceived as essentially hostile and the locus of evil and error, or at best, sometimes only of ignorance, as it always has been throughout the Age of Monologue. Rather, the outside religious and ideological world is now perceived as a possible source of knowledge, wisdom, insight, inspiration, edification —though of course one does not naively think that everything in other religions and ideologies is inspiration and wisdom. But by approaching the outside world with positive expectations, the dialogue partners are inevitably amazed at the extraordinary quantity and quality of inspiration and wisdom that is found there. They both were there all along; the monologists were deaf to them, but the dialogists—as Jesus observed of the authentic seekers among his listeners—now "have the ears to hear" (Matthew 13:9).

c) *Dialogical "Chain Reaction"*

Thirdly, the turning of one's gaze from inward to outward toward a dialogue partner creates a kind of "chain reaction." For example, the Catholic Church long was stolidly engaged in "navel staring" until the Second Vatican Council, 1962–65. In the early 1920s Pope Benedict XV refused to join with those Protestant and Orthodox Christians who invited him and Catholicism to help form the Ecumenical Movement, a movement of dialogue among Christians to work for Christian unity. His successor, Pope Pius XI, forbade Catholics to participate in the first world meeting of the Faith and Order Movement (for Christian unity) in 1927, and his successor Pope Pius XII did the same sort of thing again in 1948 and 1954.

However, his successor, "Good Pope John," Pope John XXIII, in 1959 called the Second Vatican Council "to renew the Catholic Church so it could work for Christian unity." The Council went on to officially insist on the absolute necessity of Catholics entering into dialogue not only with Protestants and Orthodox Christians, but also with Jews, Muslims, Hindus, Buddhists and other religionists and also non-believers.

Once the turn to dialogue with the first logical partners for Catholics—Protestants and Orthodox—was made, the inner logic of that turn continued the dialogic move to each next "logical" partner: If inspiration and wisdom can be found in dialogue with non-Catholic Christians, should that not also be possible with Judaism, Christianity's "source"? Why not, then, the other Semitic religion, Islam? The religions of the East, Hinduism, Buddhism, Confucianism, Taoism, etc.? Why not "All men of good will," as John XXIII put it in his moving encyclical *Pacem in terris*?

The spiritual "fission/fusion" that has occurred as a result of this "chain reaction" in the Catholic Church has indeed been nothing short of "nuclear." The Council itself stated that "All Christians should do their best to promote dialogue . . . as a duty of fraternal charity suited to our progressive and adult age."[55] In his very first encyclical (1964), Pope Paul VI wrote: "Dialogue is demanded nowadays. . . . It is demanded . . . by the maturity man has reached in this day and age."[56] In 1968 the Vatican Secretariat for Dialogue with Unbelievers wrote that, "Doctrinal dialogue should be initiated with courage and sincerity, with the greatest freedom," and added these stunning words: "Doctrinal discussion [must] recognize the truth everywhere, even if the truth demolishes one so that one is forced to reconsider one's own position, in theory and in practice."[57]

d) *Adapt Elements from Our Dialogue Partners*

Fourthly, in dialogue we will not only learn to know our partners more accurately, but also often find things in their tradition that we find admirable, even to the point that we will want to adapt certain elements from our partners for ourselves. For example, some Buddhist traditions of meditation have made a strong impression on many Christians. Conversely, some Buddhists have been greatly impressed by the Christian commitment to social justice, even to the point of going to prison or dying for social justice. The result has been that some Christians have taken up meditation methods they learned from Buddhists, and some Buddhists have become deeply involved in social justice actions.

However, interreligious dialogue should not lead to a kind of syncretism in the sense of an eclectic mixture of elements from here and there. Rather, dialogue should, and does, lead one to "adapt" rather than simply "adopt" elements from our

---

[55] Vatican II, *Decree on the Apostolate of the Laity*, n. 7.

[56] Pope Paul VI's encyclical *Ecclesiam suam*, 1964, n. 79.

[57] *Humanae personae dignitatem*, August 28, 1968, in: Austin Flannery, ed., *Vatican Council II* (Collegeville, MN: Liturgical Press, 1975), pp. 1007, 1010.

dialogue partners. This means that the adapted element is modified to fit with integrity into the first partner's tradition. For example, a Christian does not become a non-theist by adapting Zen meditation; a Buddhist does not engage in social justice action despite her/his being a Buddhist, but because of it!—as was vigorously stated by the Theravada Buddhist Sulak Sivaraksa from Bangkok.

e) *Dialogue Must Result in Practice*

Fifthly, dialogue must result in joint action in the practical area. Such joint religious action began to develop in earnest in the West only in the nineteenth century. Until that time efforts to help disadvantaged human beings were pretty much done on a remedial individualistic basis. "Charitable" institutions were founded—actually in quite extraordinary richness. The situation began to change drastically, however, with the coming of the Industrial Revolution in England in the late eighteenth century and elsewhere in Europe and America starting in the nineteenth century: the old guild and feudal systems no longer functioned for the increasing millions caught in the transfer of populations to the cities.

Whereas most people had died quite young and a much smaller population lived in relative social and geographical stability before the nineteenth century, suddenly a massive and exploding population problem burst upon the world for which neither civil society nor religion was prepared. Individual acts of charity and charitable institutions were increasingly swamped in the growing flood of social misery that rose as the nineteenth and twentieth centuries wore on. At the same time the structures of society and their workings were being studied. Plans on how to shape and re-shape those structures were laid and tested, adjusted and re-tested. Such awareness, planning and action also took place within Western religions.

Around the globe today Christian churches and Jewish synagogues spend hundreds of millions of dollars annually on social justice issues, a significant portion of which is aimed at changing the structures of society to benefit more people. The notion is spreading among Christians that the mission of the Church is to preach the Good News of the Gospel to all humanity, not just quantitatively in terms of individual persons, but also qualitatively in terms of every portion of the human beings —and the human patterns one lives in are an essential part of one's humanity. The message of the *relationality* of all reality, and very much including humankind, has struck home here.

A similar phenomenon is also beginning to take place in some dimensions of Buddhism. One very striking example is Won Buddhism, which sprang up in Korea early in the twentieth century. Clearly Won Buddhism works to combine the principles of Gautama Buddha with an affirmation of modern science and technology in working for the betterment of men and women, individually and collectively; hence, it is not surprising that the Won Buddhists also have a very strong commitment to interreligious dialogue.

There is a like development in Japan, namely, in some of the so-called "new religions" which are Buddhist based. For example, the Rissho Kosei-Kai, founded in the 1930s by Nikkyo Niwano, still alive and active at 84, was initially very much an individualistically oriented branch of Buddhism, but in recent decades—significantly as a result of dialogue with Catholics, and in particular a meeting with Pope Paul VI in 1965—it has moved to a strong commitment to social justice and interreligious dialogue.

At the same time, I would like to stress that joint religious action should not be limited to helping those who are in material need. Rather, I would like to suggest that the "other" toward whom our joint "altruistic" ethical action should reach might be named simply, the oppressed, the unfree in any dimension—and who is completely free? Logic, of course, also directs that those in greatest need should receive the greatest attention, but it likewise directs that each should contribute according to her/his gifts, and in a preeminent, though not exclusive, way to those before them *now* in need, whether that need be material, spiritual, social, esthetic or whatever: For example, producing good material things both for the well-to-do as well as the poor, teaching both the poor as well as the well-to-do, making democracy work better both for the well-to-do as well as the poor, creating beauty both for the poor as well as the well-to-do.

In the U.S., for example, the material poverty of the 30 million "poor" must be eradicated, but at the same time the various spiritual poverties of the 220 million "well-to-do" must likewise be diminished. This "preferential option for the unfree" in no way rules out the "preferential option for the poor." Rather, it includes it—in eminent fashion—but expands it.

Conclusion: Interreligious, interideological action that does not eventuate in dialogue will grow mindless, ineffective. Interreligious, interideological dialogue that does not eventuate in action will grow hypocritical, ineffective. Neither can survive singly.

f) *Probe New Questions Not Raised Before*

Sixthly, patiently pursued dialogue will eventually cast up new questions that neither of the dialogue partners had thought of on one's own. Here is the area of the greatest potential creativity in dialogue. Of course, we won't know what the creative questions will be ahead of time. If we did, they would not be new, not be fully creative. Still, let me offer two examples of such questions that have already begun to arise from the Buddhist-Christian dialogue in one case and the Christian-Muslim in the other:

i. *Effects of Describing Ultimate Reality*

Earlier I laid out something of my understanding of Christian (and one could perhaps also add here, Jewish and Muslim) and Buddhist understandings of Ultimate Reality. I, along with some other Christians engaged in dialogue with Buddhism, suggested that the Christian penchant for describing Ultimate Reality in positive terms (Being, *Pleroma*) and the Buddhist tendency to describe it in negative terms (Emptiness, *Sunyata*) need not be understood as mutually exclusive contradictions, but perhaps more like complementary descriptions.

Now, if this position is more or less accepted, it becomes extremely interesting and enlightening to investigate whether, and then how, these different descriptions of Ultimate Reality "make a difference in the world." Is the patent fact that the

Semitic religions over the centuries have invested huge energies in trying to improve the human lot *in this world*, and that Buddhism institutionally has been relatively uninterested connected with their descriptions of Ultimate Reality? Is the other indisputable fact that at least two of the Semitic religions have consistently over centuries been vastly more aggressive, intolerant and violent than has Buddhism also connected with their particular—affirmative, negative—descriptions of Ultimate Reality?

If there is a connection, what are its mechanisms? What, if anything, can, or should, be done about it? These, I believe, could be extremely critical questions for the future of humanity, of the religions in questions, and their mutual relationships.

ii. *Human Rights and Separation of Religion and State*

It was mentioned above that the biblical notion of the equal dignity of all human beings because they were all created by the one God as *imagines Dei* was one of the pillars of what is known today as Human Rights, as are enshrined in the United Nations 1948 Declaration and subsequent documents. Two other pillars are the Greek concept of the political rule of the people, democracy, and the highly developed Roman system of universal law. It took a long and circuitous evolution of human history before Western civilization was able to establish on the foundation of these three pillars the modern concept and growing reality of Human Rights. However, particularly after the American and French Revolutions at the end of the eighteenth century, Human Rights began to become a conscious reality—unfortunately often resisted by the Christian Church until recent decades, when it has become a vigorous promoter of Human Rights.

One of the essential elements in the advances of Western civilization in the area of Human Rights, as well as in science, politics in general and economic prosperity, the like of which was never before experienced in human history, is the separation of state and religion—and "religion" here of course includes any ideology that functions like a religion, as, for example, atheistic Marxism.

Western civilization in the Late Middle Ages began reaching the cultural level of the earlier Greek and Roman and the then contemporary Islamic civilizations. All historical data strongly suggest that Christendom would have plateaued at that approximate level for a longer or shorter period of time, and then gone into decline—as had all other civilizations before then, and as eventually the Islamic civilization did as well.

That did not happen, however. Why? One very fundamental reason is that, starting with the Renaissance, religion and the state slowly and very painfully began to be separated. This separation broke the forced quality of religion (ideology) and consequently freed the human spirit and mind to pursue its limitless urge to know ever more, to solve every problem it confronts. This resulted in a series of what historians call revolutions: the Commercial Revolution (16–17th centuries), Scientific Revolution (17th century), Industrial Revolution (18th century), Political Revolution (epitomized in the American and French Revolutions, 18th century), and on into the 19th and 20th centuries with myriads of revolutions of all sorts occurring at geometrically increasing speed and magnitude.

With these "exponential" advances in capabilities, of course, the possibilities of destructiveness increased correspondingly—as the medieval philosophers said: The corruption of the best becomes the worst, *Corruptio optimae pessima.* Nevertheless, because freedom is of the essence of being human, even though we may well destroy ourselves if we do not learn wisdom and live virtuously, we can never turn back to an unfree stage of human development.

Hence, those societies which try to reunite religion/ideology with the power of the state are doomed to always be third-class societies. That is why, for example, I am convinced that the present attempt of "Islamists" (Muslim term for "fundamentalists") to reestablish the Muslim law, the *Shar'ia,* in the Muslim world will condemn those countries to *always* be behind the "West." And, given the Islamists' memory of the past medieval cultural glory and superiority of Islam over the West, it is precisely the present inferiority in every way of all Islamic countries vis-à-vis the West that infuriates them.

When they argue that Islam is different from Christianity because, unlike Christianity, it is a holistic religion which includes politics as well as all other aspects of life, they need to be reminded that Christendom was exactly the same for well over a millennium—the Constantinian Era. It is only when the West broke out of that mischievous marriage of religion/ideology and state that it embarked on the path of human freedom with its limitless possibilities of creativity (and destruction).

g) *Dialogue for a Global Ethos*[58]

Seventhly, dialogue must lead to the building of a consensus on a Global Ethos; bilateral dialogues, vital as they are, are no longer sufficient for the world of today and tomorrow. By "ethos" here is meant the fundamental attitude toward good and evil, and the basic principles to carry that attitude into action.

It is beyond the borders of sanity that Catholics and Protestants are blowing each other up in Northern Ireland, that Hindus and Buddhists wantonly murder each other in Sri Lanka, that Jews and Muslims are always teetering on the abyss of war in the Near East, that Sikhs and Hindus terrorize each other in the Punjab, that in Kashmir Muslims and Hindus are always in a state of unrest, with hands on their guns, that in Afghanistan Marxists and Muslims murder each other with abandon, that various factions of Christians and Muslims have made the "Switzerland of the Near East," Lebanon, a roiling charnelhouse—and on and on. Our religions and ideologies must put a stop to these perversions of Religion and Ideology!

Though modern secular men and women often put us to shame in their human love and compassion, ultimately they may find it extremely difficult to provide a philosophical basis for such positive actions toward humans. After, all, strictly rationally just why should someone do something for one's "neighbor"? The religions, however, have profound answers to that fundamental ethical question, but they must no longer speak in multiple, confusing tongues about it.

---

[58] I am grateful to Professor Hans Küng for this programmatic insight from his new book *Projekt Weltethos* (Munich: Piper Verlag, 1990); *Global Responsibility. In Search of a New World Ethic* (New York: Crossroad, 1991). I cannot recommend its reading—and acting thereon—too highly.

A beginning has been made, of course, through organizations like the World Conference on Religion and Peace. But the occasional large-scale meeting in various places in the world is far from sufficient. The situation is much too critical and is becoming increasingly critical at an almost geometric rate of acceleration.

Horrendous as the bombings of Hiroshima and Nagasaki were (as an American of that generation I condemn them), imagine if Hitler had had a nuclear bomb with which to tip his V-2 rockets that he rained down on London (and could have most anywhere else in the world) the last months of World War II. The real horror is that he was only a few months away from his goal when the Allied armies marched into the secret laboratory in a mountain cave in the tiny southwest German village of Haigerloch in late April of 1945! The same is true of Saddam Hussein: had the Israelis not destroyed his nuclear plant in 1985 he would by 1990 have had a nuclear bomb to fit on his SCUD missiles—which, remember were fired not only at the Jews in Israel but also fellow Muslims and the Allied forces from thirty-four countries in Saudia Arabia. Further, what does he have yet in his secret arsenal? Or other ruthless men in the world?

The world does not have the luxury of waiting patiently for a Global Ethos!

i. Every major religion and ideology needs to commission its expert scholars to focus their research and reflection on articulating a Global Ethos from the perspective of their religion —in dialogue with all other religions and ideologies. Every religious and ideological institution with such experts needs to press them to use their creativity not only among themselves—that, however, is also very necessary!—but also in conjunction with expert scholars from other religious and ideological institutions.

ii. The already existing scholarly institutions of scholars of ethics (e.g., American Society of Ethics, Catholic Theological Society of America, American Academy of Religion, Academy of Jewish Philosophy) need to bring their joint resources to bear on the forging of a Global Ethos in as dialogical manner as possible.

iii. Collaborative "Working Groups," of scholars in the field of ethics which are very deliberatively interreligious, interideological need to be formed specifically to tackle this momentous task, and those which already exist (e.g., the "Annual International Scholars' Jewish-Christian-Muslim Dialogue") need to focus their energies on it.

iv. Beyond that, there needs to be a major permanent "Global Ethos Research Center" which will have some of the best experts from the world's religions and ideologies in residence, pursuing precisely this topic in its multiple ramifications. Such a project should deliberately not be funded by any one religious or ideological institution, but should have the financial support of a broad base of religions and ideologies, and the active commitment of each in urging their best experts to accept an invitation to be a resident scholar for several years at a stretch.

Such a "Global Ethos Research Center" would first of all be charged with the task of drawing together the research and reflection on global ethos and related matters into a "Universal Declaration of Global Ethos," which would then be circulated to the various forums of all the religions and ideologies, and returned to the Center for appropriate revision—with a view to eventual adoption by all the religions and ideologies of the world. Such a "Universal Declaration of Global Ethos" would then serve a function similar to the Universal Declaration of Human Rights—a kind of standard that all will be expected to live up to.

Already the several versions of the "Golden Rule" discussed above provide a starting point for such a "Universal Declaration of Global Ethos," which will have to center on care and reverence for all humans—and therefore be "anthropocentric"—but go beyond to care and reverence for all reality—and therefore really be "cosmo-anthropo-centric." The difficult problem of the differing understandings of and articulations about Ultimate Reality will also have to be resolved for incorporation in the Universal Declaration of Global Ethos—otherwise it will not be completely persuasive in the various religious and ideological communities.

After the initial period, which doubtless would last several years, the "Global Ethos Research Center" could serve as an authoritative religious and ideological scholarly locus to which always-new specific problems of global ethos could be submitted for evaluation, analysis and response. The weightiness of the responses would be "substantive," not "formal." That is, its solutions would carry weight because of their inherent persuasiveness coming from their intellectual and spiritual insight and wisdom.

Such an undertaking by the religions and ideologies of the world would be different from, but complementary to, the work of the United Nations. The UN brings to bear the political force of all the nations of the world on the manifold problems of the globe. The "Global Ethos Research Center" would in a major way bring to bear the moral and spiritual force of all the religions and ideologies of the world on many of those same problems, as well as those that are not easily susceptible to political force.

3. *Interim Conclusion II*

In conclusion, humankind needs an "explanation of the ultimate meaning of life, and an ethics of how to live accordingly." Every religion tries to provide such an explanation and ethics based on a notion of the Transcendent; an ideology attempts to do the same not based on a notion of the Transcendent. While the inherent variety of humankind, stemming from human freedom, assures that there will always be a variety of "explanations and ethics," a variety of religions and ideologies, these religions and ideologies can no longer continue to exist in hostility toward, or isolation from, each other. Rather, they all need to expand and deepen their understanding of reality, including Ultimate Reality, by learning from each other, by being in dialogue. Most pressing of all is the need for this dialogue to focus on the building of a Global Ethos.

IV. CONTEMPORARY CHRISTIANITY'S CONTRIBUTION

What can Christianity in particular offer to the world now at the edge of the Third Millennium as we are entering the Age of Dialogue? It has something at once very old and very new. In brief, what Third Millennium Christianity has to offer is a result of a major paradigm shift that has taken place in Christianity in recent decades, and in fact is still going on. This is the shift, as we have seen to some extent, from a static, ideological, exclusivistic view of religion and the world to one that is dynamic, pragmatic, dialogic. This has meant the embracing of modern critical methods of thinking as the essential means of reappropriating the tradition. As with all creative renewal movements, contemporary Christianity is also in the process of returning to its source, not in a romantic spirit, but as a necessary step to make its source once again vital in today's world. It is that Source, "revitalized," made newly, more profoundly, available through contemporary methods, that Christianity can offer the world for the third millennium.

1. *Return to Sources*

The source, the origin, of Christianity—despite its name—is not "the Christ," not the Church, not the New Testament, but Jesus (Yeshua, as he was called in Hebrew) the Jew, his thought, teaching and living example, that is, what Yeshua "thought, taught and wrought."

Millions of Christians have for centuries focussed their main attention on something other than the source of Christianity. They focussed on a religious/theological concept, "Christ," the "Anointed One," which was laden with all sorts of meanings beyond its original Jewish meaning of a man who was given special responsibilities by God—and hence also powers to carry out those responsibilities. Or they focussed on the doctrinal teachings of the Church as laid out in early universal (Ecumenical) Councils, or by the Pope. Or they focussed on the writings of the Bible, especially the New Testament.

However, none of those are the source of Christianity. The source of Christianity is Yeshua of Nazareth (whose family name was not "Christ"), who himself was not a Christian, who did not read the New Testament, who indeed did not even found a Church. Rather, he was a devout Jew whose "family name," if he had had one, would have been "Ben-Yosep" (Josephson) or "ha Notzri" (the Nazarene) who read the Hebrew Bible, and as a "Rabbi" gathered around him a band of Jewish followers to be sent to "the children of the House of Israel," as did other rabbis.

It is to that source, to Jesus of Nazareth, "Yeshua ha Notzri," that more and more Christians are turning at the present time, both as individuals—ordinary people and theologians—and as ecclesiastical institutions. And it is also precisely that source, Yeshua, that has much to offer the world in the Third Millennium.

2. *Yeshua: A Concrete Human Being*

The first thing to notice about the source of Christianity, Yeshua, is that it is not an abstraction, not a set of ideas or teachings, not an ideology—but a concrete person. Of course ideas and wise teachings are important, even essential, but in unembodied form they have limited inspirational power by which women and men can set their lives. The thin power of an ideology by itself is borne out time and again by the examples of some of the seemingly most powerful ideologies desperately casting up human figures as the centers of inspiration. Why else, for example, the wax-like preserved bodies of Lenin and Mao Zedong in Red Square and Tiananmen Square, to say nothing of the millions of pictures and statues of them scattered about?

The most fetching thing about Yeshua is that he lived—and died—his profound teachings. It is one thing to teach the love of one's neighbor as oneself, as is taught in the Hebrew Bible. It is quite something more to pour out one's life helping person after person, no matter how wretched and unattractive they are—even to love one's enemies to the point of dying with a plea of forgiveness for them on one's lips. This is the stuff of which enduring human inspiration is made. Such a person will be an inspiration, a model for life, as long as there are human beings and his life's story is placed in front of them.

This very strength, of course, automatically carries with it a great danger. In the warmth of that extraordinary life, people will want to give expression to the deep emotions it stirs within them. They will want to say the very best they can imagine about him. And so, many miraculous acts will often be attributed to him, and increasingly so. This can be seen happening in the four canonical Christian Gospels, and with even greater intensity and imagination in the later apocryphal gospels.

But these alleged preter- and super-natural dimensions attached to Yeshua are not what will be helpful to the contemporary world; they in fact will serve, as they have in past Christian history, more as distractions, if they are taken literally. Rather, they need to be—not simply thrown out but—"demythologized" and brought up to the level of the "second naivete," where they will be appreciated for the deeply meaningful poetic metaphors and symbols that they truly are, thereby pointing to a deeper reality that can not be captured in purely prose articulation.

It is already enough of a "mind-blowing" image to see a man who so takes to heart the profound Jewish insight into the meaning of living an authentic human life by "loving one's neighbor AS oneself" that he lives it out minute by minute, person by person. Yeshua does that, but also more:

It was noted before that just as the object of knowing, of the cognitive faculty, is the "true," so the object of loving, of the affective faculty, is the "good," and that one thus wants to be united with the "good," in some appropriate way, whether it is to eat a "good" ice cream cone, to have a "good," comfortable house, to be with a "good" person, as one's friend. Said other, love is a unitive force; when we love another person, that means that we become more and more one with the other person, the beloved, and we then also want to unite the other "goods" that we perceive in the world with our "other self," our *alter ego*, the beloved.

Now, as already pointed out, Jews and Christians are taught to love all human beings as themselves. But often they must do so, if they in fact do it, by a sheer act of the will: I know in my mind that I should love, should will the "good" for, this unattractive person before me. What comes across in the image of Yeshua, however, is that he truly "loved" even his enemies, that is, he was able to *see* the goodness in them, no matter how deeply it may have been covered over, and move to draw other good to those persons—not because he *believed* they held an inner goodness somewhere, but because he *knew* that goodness—and acted accordingly.

Here, then, is a person who will accept me regardless of my failures, no matter how low I sink morally, psychologically, physically, or however—not because I *presumably* possess some goodness, some lovableness, but because I in fact really have it, even though I at times might despair of locating it. No matter what, here is someone with whom I am "at home" (it is said that "home" is where they have to take you in—no matter what!).

But such a human "friend" with whom one can feel so at home necessarily motivates one to imitation. It is sometimes remarked that imitation is the highest type of compliment—and it is. It is also true that those we admire the most are automatically also the ones we try to imitate the most. Hence, the deep, open-to-all love felt in Yeshua necessarily moves the person thus loved to similarly love in an open-to-all manner. Such a force is of immense power in human life. And it is this force that Christianity has to offer the contemporary world: the concrete human Yeshua who *lived* his love of each person regardless of who they were.

3. *Yeshua: Positive on Life*

One of the banes of the two thousand year Christian tradition is the massive infection it has suffered from extreme dualism, that is, that view which in brief says: Body is bad and spirit is good. It can be found to some extent already in the later New Testament writings in its growing subordination of women, who soon thereafter are increasingly depicted in Christianity as "the devil's gateway" (Tertullian, 2nd century), the "bringer of death into the world" (*Vita Adam et Evae*, 2nd century).

The extreme Christian asceticism found in strength already in the second century was another reflection of this extreme dualism, which entered Christianity not from Yeshua or his Jewish religious culture, but from Hellenistic culture, which was rife with extreme dualisms of all sorts. Even in Plato one can see the effects of this dualistic attitude: The body, which is mortal, is understood as the prison of the soul, which alone is immortal; our sense knowledge is only of a shadow of the true reality, the Idea.

Such an extreme dualist view, however, runs fundamentally contrary to the Bible's view of reality as it is laid out in its very beginning when the creation of the world is described. The Hebrews made an extraordinary breakthrough in human history in seeing the unity of the cosmos: They claimed that the various parts of reality did not come into existence under the aegis of various gods or spirits or disparate forces, but rather, all reality had a single source—Yahweh God, the only creator of all. The crown of God's creation was Humanity (*ha Adam*, literally, "the earthling") who was created from matter (*Adamah*, earth or soil) with a divine element, breath or spirit (*Ruach*) from God, breathed into it. Hence, for the Hebrews a human was not two separate realities temporally juxtaposed, a body and a spirit, but an embodied spirit, or enspirited body—a "body-spirit."

Beyond that, the Hebrews also wrestled with the problem of evil in a creative way: In the Genesis story of creation (the whole story of course is properly understood as a profound myth explaining reality, and hence, if it is taken with true seriousness, it must be perceived as such—Paul Ricoeur's level of "second naivete") at the end of each day it states that God saw that what he had done was good (*tov*); at the end of creation, on the sixth day, it says that God saw that all that he had done was very good (*mod tov*).

There were no evil gods or spirits who created evil things, as was often explained by other ancient, polytheistic or animistic, peoples. Rather, evil came into the world by humanity's not following the structural laws Yahweh God had built into humanity at creation: In following the deception of the serpent, humanity freely chose to try to "be like God" in deciding what was good and evil (eating the forbidden fruit of the tree of the knowledge of good and evil). Here was the first "domino theory," that is, when humanity fell out of "order" in its relationship to Yahweh God, its relationship with the rest of creation also fell into disorder in a kind of chain reaction. (This is the symbolic meaning of the "curses" leveled against Adam and Eve as they are driven from the Garden of Eden; the "curses" were not really punishments God visited on humans, but rather what humans did to themselves, like degenerative diseases resulting from environmental pollution.)

The main point to observe here, however, is that everything is created by Yahweh God, and it is created *tov*, indeed, *mod tov*! This is the Jewish tradition within which Yeshua and all his first followers lived: He enjoyed friends; he ate—even after the "resurrection event"! He drank wine; he even made it! He was in this regard very different from Siddhartha Gautama, the Buddha, who taught his followers that fundamentally all life is suffering or sorrow, *dukkha*. Rather, Yeshua said to his followers: "I have come that you may have life, and have it more abundantly!" (John 10:10).

To be sure, Yeshua did not live a suffering-free life. Where Gautama lived to old age and died of "natural" causes, Yeshua died a violent, excruciatingly (note the word!—*crux*, cross) painful death—and he overcame it not by fleeing it, but by accepting it fully and plunging through it to a fuller life (the "resurrection event") for himself and others.

Of course, in the teachings of Gautama the Buddha there is great wisdom and "salvific" energy. Rightly understood, Buddhist doctrine is not world-fleeing and pessimistic, as it might seem to be at first blush. Nevertheless, it must be granted that in trying to "sell" Buddhism—and a teaching that isn't "bought" by people surely is worthless to them—the beginning idea that "all life is *dukkha*" would not exactly be an advertising manager's dream slogan! Perhaps, however, in a culture like India's with its massive population and even more massive poverty such a "slogan" did find a deep resonance in reality, if not great enthusiasm.

To continue the comparison with Buddhism for a moment longer, Buddhism penetrated deeply into Chinese culture and life, but as it did it in turn was also profoundly shaped by China, especially by China's sense of practicality and concern for correct action in this world. Now it is precisely this pragmatism and this-worldliness, this humanism, that provides a striking parallel with the fundamental optimism and ethics-orientation of the Jewish tradition, with Yeshua at the heart of it. We are not talking here of the Augustinian and subsequent mis-reading of Paul's teaching about being "saved by faith," but about the teaching and life of Yeshua, who among other things described the "Last Judgment" as based on whether a person has given food to the hungry, drink to the thirsty, clothes to the naked, etc., even when they are "the least important of people" (Matthew 25:31–46).

To repeat: Without fleeing from suffering, Yeshua's view of life is thoroughly optimistic. God has created all humans good. Though they may have wandered into one kind or another confusion, or even slavery, they can find their way (which, as noted, is what the first followers of the teachings of Yeshua called themselves—not Christians, but followers of "The Way") back to a properly ordered life, to the "Reign of

God," wherein the laws God structured into humans are again followed. Further, the core of God's laws are the Two Great Commandments: 1) love of God, which can be fulfilled only through 2) love of one's neighbors as oneself—and one's neighbors most in need of love are the "least important of people."

4. *Yeshua's Question: What Must I Do?*

Yeshua was a Jew, and for Jews the big question was not, "What must I think?" That was the big question for the Greeks. The Greeks, after all, were the ones who invented the science of abstract rational thinking, as our vocabulary tells us: philosophy (*philo-sophia*), logic (*logos*), metaphysics (*meta-physikos*), ontology (*ontos-logos*). It was the Greek Christians who developed the highly speculative doctrines of Christianity: Christology, Trinity, etc. Indeed, it was they who spelled out the primary essence of Christianity in creeds, the long lists of the precise way members must think. Again our vocabulary reveals this to us, for we speak of the members of Christianity as "believers," that is, those who believe, who think, a certain way. The technical term the Catholic Code of Canon Law uses to refer to Church members is just that, "Believers in Christ," *Christfideles*.

As a Jew, the big question for Yeshua was, "What must I do?" His great concern was not doctrine, but ethics. There are no "creeds" in Judaism. It has only the regularly repeated prayer, the *Shema Israel*: "Hear, O Israel! Yahweh our God is one" (Deuteronomy 6:4). The burden of Judaism is expressed in the phrase "ethical monotheism," for if there is only one God who created everything, there is only one "order" or code of ethics that God has structured into all creation. Thus it is the *Torah*, God's Instructions (often badly translated as Law), that holds the pride of place in Judaism.

As noted before, just as the early followers (note the word!) of Yeshua designated themselves as followers of the "Way" (*Hodos*) to live a proper human life as taught and exemplified by Yeshua, so also the followers of what became known as Rabbinic Judaism placed the "Way" (*Halacha*) at the center of their tradition, and that other Semitic religion, Islam, as well placed the "Way" (*Shar'ia*) at its center, and likewise the Indian religions, Hinduism (*Marga*) and Buddhism (*Magga*), and the Chinese religions (*Tao*). In this regard the focus of Yeshua and Christianity fits well with and reenforces the heart of the other great religions of the world.

There are, of course, many specifics that are involved in deciding the correct "Way" to act in specific circumstances, but, as seen earlier, for Yeshua as a Jew the core of the Way was summed up in the Two Great Commandments: 1) loving God wholly, which is concretely carried out by 2) loving one's neighbor AS oneself. One can love one's neighbor only to the extent that one loves oneself authentically. The "Golden Rules" of Hillel, Yeshua—and Confucius and other religious traditions—also start with a love of self as the basis for loving the other: "Do unto others AS you would have them do unto you." If you do not truly love yourself, you cannot love others: As the Christian medieval scholars noted, you can't give what you don't have: *Nemo dat quod non habet.*

a) *A Further Analysis of the Meaning of Love*

As noted before, and here summarized and put in somewhat more detailed Aristotelian categories: Just as the object of the intellect, the highest human cognitive faculty, is the true, the object of the will, the highest human appetitive faculty, is the good. As the cognitive faculty moves outwardly-inwardly, reaching out to draw the outside world into itself by knowing it, thereby "becoming one" with it, so too the appetitive faculty moves outwardly-inwardly, reaching out to draw the outside world into itself by loving it, thereby "becoming one" with it. The very structure of the appetitive faculty is to reach out toward what the cognitive faculty presents as the true/good, to draw it to itself, thereby moving to become one with it. Thus the fundamental meaning of the term love is, having perceived the good, to reach out to draw it to oneself, to thus become one with it.

At the same time, however, loving oneself is only the first

half of the basic move toward humanization, as I argued elsewhere[59] when presenting mutuality as an essential element in self-transcendence, the becoming unendingly ever more fully human. Thus, true self-love for humans implies that they move endlessly toward becoming more fully themselves, i.e., more wholly human—which can be done only by moving beyond oneself, by knowing and loving the other. Consequently, just as I cannot love others if I do not truly love myself, so also I cannot truly love myself if I do not love others. If I do not move out to know and love others, I will not become fully human, and if I do not move to become fully human, I will not be truly reaching out for the greatest good for myself as a human—I will not be truly loving myself.

To turn once again to more detailed abstract Aristotelian terms: The nature of the will is to draw the good to itself, to identify with it. In this process I will become more or less identified with other centers of consciousness, with other persons. As mentioned above, when this love identification becomes strong enough, we speak of the beloved becoming my *alter ego*, my other self. Now my love takes the form of drawing the good not only to my "first" *ego*, but also to my *alter ego*, and if the love identification is sufficiently intense I might draw the good to my *alter ego* rather than my "first" *ego* so entirely that I might even give up the greatest good in my "first" *ego* for the sake of giving it to my *alter ego*: "Greater love than this has no one than that they give up their life for their friend" (John 15:13). It should be obvious, however, that this "altruism" is not in conflict with an authentic "egoism," for in this case the "*alter*" is the "*ego*."

This, however, is the last, the highest stage of human development, the stage of the (w)holy person, the saint, the arahat, the bodhisattva, the sage. As noted before, such a stage cannot be the *foundation* of human society, rather, it must be the *goal*

---

[59] Leonard Swidler, *After the Absolute: The Dialogical Future of Religious Reflection* (Minneapolis: Fortress Press, 1990).

of it; the foundation of human society must first be self-love, which of course necessarily includes moving outward to loving others.

It is precisely this initial self-love necessarily moving outward to loving others embedded in the heart of Judaism that Yeshua taught as the foundation of the whole Jewish tradition.

b) *Both Judaism and Christianity are Religions of Love*

It has long been a vicious Christian canard that Judaism is merely, and harshly, a religion of law and justice, whereas Christianity, following Yeshua, is a religion of love. In fact, Yeshua made it clear that there was no split between the two—justice/law and love. Rather, they were one. As noted above, he summed up his understanding of religion as the following of the twofold command or law: To love God and neighbor. This, however, was nothing new. Yeshua was simply quoting from the ancient Torah, Deuteronomy 6:5, indeed, a portion of the opening of the Jewish daily prayer, the *Shema*: "Love the Lord your God with all your heart, with all your soul, and with all your strength," and Leviticus 19:18: "Love your neighbor as you love yourself."

Moreover, the linking together of these two commandments and the summing up of the Law (*Torah*) in them was not something new or special to Yeshua. According to Luke 10:25–28, it was an "expert in the law" in the crowd who spoke of the twofold command of love; Yeshua merely agreed with him. Further, perhaps two hundred years before Yeshua was born, other Jewish writers stated much the same sentiments. They are found in various of the Pseudepigrapha (non-canonical Jewish writings in Greek): "Love the Lord and the neighbor" (*Testament of Issachar* 5:2); "I loved the Lord and every human being with my whole heart" (ibid., 7:6); "Love the Lord in your whole life and one another with a sincere heart" (*Testament of Daniel* 5:3); "Fear the Lord and love the neighbor" (*Testament of Benjamin* 3:3); "And he commanded them to keep to the way of God, do justice, and everyone love his/her neighbor" (*Jubilees* 20:9); "Love one another my sons as brothers, as one loves oneself. . . . You should love one another as yourselves" (ibid., 36:4–6).

Precisely the same summing up of the Law, Torah, in the double commandment of love was expressed by a Jewish contemporary of Yeshua, Philo of Alexandria (c. 20 B.C.E.–50 C.E.). In the tractate, "Concerning Individual Commandments," II,63, he wrote: "There are, so to speak, two fundamental teachings to which the numberless individual teachings and statements are subordinated: in reference to God the commandment of honoring God and piety, in reference to humanity that of the love of humanity and justice."

Obviously, Judaism was, and is, a religion of love of God and neighbor; that is the religious air that the devout Jew Yeshua breathed, and passed on to his followers—and it is there now for the whole world to accept and make its own.

c) *Christianity, Confucianism and Love: A Dialogue*

I would like to draw a dialogue parallel with another world religion, Confucianism, and observe that this lived insight of Judaism and Yeshua confirms a similar insight found in the Confucian understanding that the foundation of all love is self-love.

In Confucianism the context within which this issue is discussed is whether learning to be human—the essential human act according to Confucianism—is to be done "for the sake of others" (*wei-ren*) or "for the sake of self" (*wei-chi*—Confucius, *Analects*, 14,25). Theoretically, learning to be human can be done for both reasons: "Indeed, this preference for the inclusive 'both-and' rather than the exclusive 'either-or' solution for conflicts between self and society is a distinctive feature of Confucian ethics." However, although learning for the sake of others may appear altruistic, Confucius criticized it as inauthentic: "A decision to turn our attention inward to come to terms with our inner self, the true self, is the precondition for embarking on the spiritual journey of ultimate self-transformation. Learning for the sake of the self is the authentic way of learning to be fully human."[60]

In this foundation of self-love moving outward to loving others, Confucianism ("All men are brothers within the four seas"—Confucius, *Analects* 12, 5) and Christianity ("If you have done it to one of these least ones, you have done it to me"—Matthew 25:40) are fundamentally at one. It should be further recalled that from Confucius on the Chinese religious tradition placed the human person in the center of its concerns; the central virtue was *Ren*, kindness, compassion, or humaneness. In this connection, as we saw, Confucius taught a form of the Golden Rule, and his most famous "follower," Mencius, remarked that "the man who possessed *Ren* loved others" (*Book of Mencius* 4B, 28). Mencius even uttered something like Yeshua's startling mandate to love one's enemies when he said, "The good person treats the unloved as he does the loved" (*Mencius* 7B, 1).

However, at the same time, for Confucius an equally critical virtue was that of *Li*, understood as hierarchical order. At the heart of the Confucian understanding of what it means to be human is the idea of the five hierarchical relationships: 1) Ruler and minister, 2) father and son, 3) husband and wife, 4) older and younger brother, and 5) friend and friend. The prime paradigm was the relationship of father to son; everything else was modeled after it. The essence of the relationship was that of superior-inferior. One was to love one's fellow human being, but in the proper manner, in the correct hierarchical order. In contrast to this understanding of *Ren* was the view of a somewhat younger Chinese thinker, Mo-tzu (fifth century B.C.E.), who taught a love of all without distinction.

There is clearly a great dissimilarity between the under-

---

[60] Tu Wei-ming, "On Confucian Religiousness," pp. 40f. William Theodore de Bary, *The Liberal Tradition in China*. (Hong Kong/New York: Chinese University Press/Columbia University Press, 1983). De Bary, *Liberal Tradition in China*, p. 21, also documents thoroughly that this is indeed the position of Confucius and the Confucian tradition.

standing of the love of one's fellow human being by Yeshua and by Confucius. The former is at least egalitarian, with a special bent toward loving those who are the powerless, the oppressed of society, in keeping with the great prophetic tradition of Judaism. The latter is definitely hierarchical, with a bent toward the powerful, the potential oppressors of society.

At the same time it must be granted that there is also a great similarity between the Confucian *Li* and the Hellenistic Household Codes, as they are found in the early Christian Church: Citizens, be subject to the emperor; slaves, be subject to your masters; wives, be subject to your husbands; children, be subject to your parents. Insofar as Christianity is based not on the teaching and example of the Jew Yeshua, on what he thought, taught and wrought, as the basic touchstone for all Christian belief and praxis, but on other parts of the New Testament, especially the Stoic patriarchal hierarchism found in the deutero-Pauline and pseudo-Petrine letters (e.g., Ephesians 5:21–6:6; Colossians 3:18–22; 1 Timothy 6:1–2; Titus 2:9–10, 3:1–3; 1 Peter 2:13–14, 3:1–2, 5:5), there is also a great similarity between Confucianism and Christianity as well.

However, it appears that the Mo-tzu doctrine of egalitarian love of neighbor was successfully resisted in the subsequent development of the Confucian tradition in a way that the Yeshua teaching was not successfully resisted in the Christian tradition, especially after the eighteenth-century Enlightenment when Yeshua's sense of egalitarian love has become more and more prominent.

It must also be added that today there are vital signs that certain strains of the contemporary "New Confucianism"—which is struggling to rise like a phoenix from the ashes of the old Confucianism which went down in flames in a series of twentieth-century Chinese revolutions—are moving in directions that are attempting to radically transform *Li* away from its initial and traditional hierarchical structure toward a fundamentally "liberal, solitary and egalitarian" form.

For example, "properly interpreted in the anthropocosmic perspective, the sense of rootedness reminds us that we are responsible not only for those who came before us and brought about our existence but also for those who are yet to come";

Confucian principles are "not conservative ideas designed to maintain existing power relationships," but rather "their service of such political aims in the past was derivative of a more fundamental concern: the concern for the cosmos as a whole . . . ecological principles." In fact, "Filial piety and reverence are not conservative but conservationist ideas."[61]

Only the future will reveal the success of these efforts to incorporate into the Confucian "conservationist ideas" the modern Western turn toward freedom and the individual with Yeshua's very Jewish egalitarian love of neighbor at his foundation. They will, among other things, have to take seriously the scathing criticisms of Chinese scholars like Ze Hua Liu and Quan Ge who conclude that "Individuation is a necessary component of the full development of the human being, but Confucians only provided humanity with the procedure of socialization. . . . Following the Confucian way of human development, there was, and will be, no hope of establishing the position of the individual, his and her dignity, freedom and independence."[62] In the end, Julia Ching insists, "Confucianism can remain genuine and viable only as one value system among others, in a society where freedom and responsibility are esteemed,"[63] and I would add: where Yeshua's ancient prophetic Jewish sense of egalitarian love of neighbor, especially the oppressed, is brought to the fore.

---

[61] Tu Wei-ming, "On Confucian Religiousness," paper delivered at the International Confucian-Christian Conference in Hong Kong, June 8–15, 1988, p. 24—a revised and enlarged version of chapter five, "Centrality and Commonality: An Essay on Confucian Religiousness," in his forthcoming book, *Centrality and Commonality: An Essay on Chung-yung* to be published by the State University of New York.

[62] See Ze Hua Liu and Quan Ge, "On the 'Human' in Confucianism," forthcoming in the *Journal of Ecumenical Studies* for a negative critique of Confucianism as a possible basis for a democratic society. Both authors are professors at Nankai University, Tianjin, China. Professor Liu has also for several years been the Chair of the History Department, but because of his involvement in the Democracy Movement in spring 1989 he has been suspended from that position, though it has not been filled by anyone else yet.

[63] Julia Ching in, Hans Küng and Julia Ching, *Christentum und chinesische Religion* (Munich: Piper Verlag, 1988), pp. 115 f.

5. *Yeshua's Focus: On Persons*

First and last, primarily and ultimately, Yeshua was interested in persons, paralleling the Two Great Commandments, that is, loving the Ultimate Person, and all human persons. In this, Yeshua was once again quintessentially Jewish. Not only were all humans created by the one God, but they were also created as an image of God, *Imago Dei*, meaning that, like God, humans could know and freely decide/love. Thus there was only one set of ethics by which one was to treat all humans, regardless of what country they came from.

In the ancient polytheistic world, religion—an "explanation of the ultimate meaning of life, and how to live accordingly"—provided people with the ethics by which to treat their fellow religionists; but people from other countries had a different religion, a different god, and hence were not treated by the ethics the first group received from their god. Not so with the monotheistic Hebrews: There was only one God who created all humans, and therefore there was only one ethics by which to treat all humans.

How were humans to be treated in the Hebrew tradition? With the greatest of reverence, because they were created not only from the earth but also because they had a divine element, the Spirit (*Ruach*) in them, and even further, they are created in the image of God; they are all *Imagines Dei*. As noted before, here then is the foundational pillar of the modern notion of human rights: ALL humans are to be treated with the respect due to their dignity: "All human beings are born free and equal in dignity and rights. They are endowed with reason and conscience and should act towards one another in a spirit of brotherhood" (*Universal Declaration of Human Rights*, United Nations, 1948).

a) *Yeshua's Personalism*

For Yeshua it is preeminently persons who count. He spends the whole of his public life helping persons. He is obviously not interested in accumulating wealth, or in building a political power base, or in pursuing academic or scholarly interests for the sake of the abstract idea of knowledge, or in establishing and furthering an institution. He spends his energy helping individual persons in their physical and spiritual infirmities. His time is taken up constantly either in healing or in teaching persons the wisdom of life—the latter particularly through the many stories he related.

He broke many taboos to help persons. For example, he healed on the Sabbath, though some legalists criticized him for thus violating the Sabbath rule of rest. But his response was that "The Sabbath was made for humanity, not humanity for the Sabbath" (Mark 2:27).

b) *Yeshua's Feminism*

Again, when Yeshua once visited an important Pharisee he permitted a woman of ill-repute to kiss his feet, out of remorse, to wash them with her tears and wipe them with her hair—a shockingly scandalous allowance! But Yeshua dismissed what he considered the pseudo-scandal by noting that the guilt of her past misdeeds was obliterated "because she has loved much" (Luke 7:47). It was not societal custom or one's public image that was important, but persons. Persons needed to be treated with respect and love—regardless of their place in society, for all were *Imagines Dei.*

This last example points to a very special and very active concern Yeshua had for the largest of the world's oppressed classes in all cultures—women. Elsewhere I have analyzed in great detail the "feminism" Yeshua exhibited in a very patriarchal society.[64] The first extraordinary thing is that in the midst of his patriarchal society there is not recorded a single negative action or remark by Yeshua about women; the second is that there is a plethora of positive examples of Yeshua's treating women as at least the equal of men, and of his often taking stands, breaking taboos, working to free women from the shackles that bound them in that culture.

---

[64] See "Jesus Was a Feminist," first published in *The Catholic World*, January, 1971, and in at least thirty-two other places in at least six languages through 1987; and *Biblical Affirmation of Women* (Philadelphia: Westminster Press, 1979); and *Yeshua: A Model for Moderns* (Kansas City, MO: Sheed & Ward, 1988).

On this account traps were set to discredit him, either with the women he was championing or with the Jewish authorities, as in the account of the woman taken in adultery (John 8:2–11).[65] There is even documentary evidence that Yeshua was denounced to the Roman Governor Pontius Pilate because "he was leading the women astray"![66]

This teaching, and even more, this moving, lived example, of concern for individual persons regardless of their place in society as the supreme principle of behavior can be a great gift to the world in the Third Millennium.

6. *For Yeshua Ultimate Reality Is Personal: Implications*

Most of us human beings most of the time simply live in the present and on the surface of experience. However, that is not when we are most human. Rather, practically all of us have times when we glimpse some meaning beyond the surface experience. We have many ways of talking about this perception. We speak of a deeper meaning, about higher goals, of the super-natural, of heaven above, about something beyond history, about eschatology, of a meaning below the surface. In brief, we are persuaded that there is something more to reality than what meets the eye; that is the whole meaning of "meaning"—relating empirical data to the knowing subject.

With maturation we become increasingly aware of the inter-relatedness of things, including most meaningfully, relatedness with the Source and Goal of all things, Ultimate

---

[65] The facts that this story cannot be found in the earliest manuscripts and that it obviously is linguistically out of place in its present place in John's Gospel—it really was torn out of Luke's Gospel and "wandered" about until it found a home in John—make it clear that the early Christian Church (which had become so full of extreme dualism and therefore was anti-sex and misogynist) had great difficulty in accepting such an accepting attitude toward sex and women on the part of Yeshua.

[66] Marcion (2nd century) attests to the text: *kai apostrephonta tas gynaikas*, cited in Eberhard Nestle, ed., *Novum Testamentum Graece et Latine* (Stuttgart, 1954), p. 221, and Roger Gryson, *The Ministry of Women in the Early Church* (Collegeville, MN: Liturgical Press, 1976), p. 126.

Reality, however understood. Some persons eventually reach what various Eastern religious traditions, as we have seen, call Enlightenment, Awakening or Liberation or what in Christianity is sometimes referred to as Infused Contemplation.

It must be recalled that Yeshua lived in a culture that did not use abstract, philosophical thought categories and language. Rather, the ancient Semitic culture thought and spoke in "picture-language." Hence, we must not look for what is not there in the biblical texts, that is, an attempt at philosophical clarity.

a) *A Philosophical Analysis of Language*

Moreover, as was pointed out before, even when more philosophically trained thinkers speak in the most precise categories and terms possible, when they speak of Ultimate Reality, their language always falls short. For human language is necessarily based on human experience, which is always limited—but in this case it is attempting to speak of the Unlimited. Adequacy and accuracy are obviously impossible.

Perhaps the closest one can come to speaking intelligibly about Ultimate Reality is consciously to speak in what Thomas Aquinas refers to as analogical language. Thus, we could speak of both John and Mary as persons; here the term person is employed univocally, that is, with identically the same meaning. Before the consciousness of sexist language was raised, one could speak of John being a man and Mary being a man (meaning a human being), and also of John being a man and Mary not being a man (meaning a male); here the term man is used equivocally, that is, with completely different meanings. One can speak of God as person, meaning that God has the qualities of those human persons we know (ability to know and love), but without any of their limitations; here the term person is used analogously, that is, the divine person and human persons are neither identical nor completely different, but similar or analogous to each other.

This is perhaps not a terribly satisfactory way of speaking of something so terribly important, but, given our human limitations, it is probably the best we humans can do. At the same time, we must also be extremely cautious that we not fall into the trap of taking our statements about Ultimate Reality literally, thereby succumbing to idolatry (as mentioned earlier, mistaking the *idol*, the image—here, the words—for the reality it is symbolizing or pointing to).

b) *Non-Personal Understanding of Ultimate Reality*

As a Jew, Ultimate Reality for Yeshua was not simply an impersonal principle or force. Rather, Ultimate Reality is Person, that is, knowing and freely deciding/loving Reality. This understanding has been largely held throughout Christianity, and Judaism and Islam and many other religions as well, and, as was pointed out, is usually designated by the term theism, that is, belief in a personal God.

However, there is also the strand in the Judeo-Christian tradition which speaks of God in non-personal terms. To begin with, there are various non-personal metaphors for God both in the Bible and in tradition: E.g., God is the rock of my salvation, is a mighty fortress, etc. However, no one takes these metaphors to mean that God really is a rock or a fortress; these are just symbols in a very primary sense, and the terms are used very nearly equivocally, though analogously also in a somewhat extended sense.

Nevertheless, there are also those Christians, especially the mystics, who likewise speak of God in non-personal terms, used in a quite primarily analogous manner. This is particularly true when some use either very abstract or negative terms. As we saw earlier, Meister Eckhart, for example, speaks of Ultimate Reality as *Deitas* (*Gottheit*, misleadingly transliterated into English as "Godhead," whereas it ought to be "Godhood"), as *das Nichts*, "Nothingness," and as the *Ungrund*, "Abyss." The latter two mean, at least, that Ultimate Reality is so completely limitless that it is unfathomable, bottomless. Thus, often the "Way" of the mystics is called a *Via negativa*, a "negative way." Such language seems to appear among Christian mystics only at the highest reaches, or the deepest recesses (depending on which directional image one wants to use), and appears to be a reflection of the experience of the finite encountering the Infinite; concepts and language necessarily fall far short and one is reduced to stuttering negatives.

Now this part of the Christian tradition fits quite well with the negative descriptions of Ultimate Reality as found in the East, especially in Buddhism and some forms of Taoism. Taking up the former, Ultimate Reality is spoken of in Mahayana Buddhism as the Void, Emptiness, *Sunyata*. However, upon investigation it becomes clear, as has been seen, that *Sunyata* is not meant as merely the absence of being, but is understood in a much more dynamic sense, as the Zen Buddhist Master Masao Abe quoted earlier indicates.

Perhaps an analogy will help—so long as one remembers that it is just an analogy, and therefore is not to be followed where it no longer is helpful—*Omnia analogia claudet.* That Ultimate Reality is Emptiness, *Sunyata*, means that "ultimately" it has no specific form. Hence, it is like the energy (*Dynamis* in Greek) of electricity when it is still in the dynamo; it does not yet have any specific form: neither the form of light (in lamps), nor heat (in stoves), nor locomotion (in trains). The unspecified electrical energy in the dynamo is like Ultimate Reality in that it is the source of the specific "being" or forms of electricity as light, heat, locomotion, but is itself without any form, is, as Masao Abe put it, "Formless Emptiness," or "Boundless Openness."

c) *Personal Understanding of Ultimate Reality*

In any case, Christians can accept the non-personal manner of speaking of Ultimate Reality, but they are not likely to give up the personal way of speaking of Ultimate Reality in addition, for at least two, possibly three, reasons:

One is that it is so centrally and fundamentally fixed in the Christian tradition from the very beginning, in the words of Yeshua and the Jewish texts and tradition before him.

A second is that the principle of sufficient cause recommends retaining it. That is, there must be a sufficient cause for the existence of something. For example, if a large crater were found, no one would be satisfied with the explanation that it resulted from the explosion of one gram of TNT; there would have to be a much larger amount, or its explosive equivalent, to account for, to provide a "sufficient cause" for, the existence of the crater.

Now in fact knowing and loving beings, persons, exist; therefore there must be a source of such "perfection" of being which will be a sufficient cause, which will mean having at least the perfection of what humans know as "personhood." Hence Ultimate Reality must be at least personal, or perhaps better said, supra-personal or trans-personal—but not less than personal, and therefore not just non-personal.

A third reason is that the vast majority of humans seem to psychologically need to perceive and relate to Ultimate Reality as personal. This is very obvious in Buddhism, which although in its original teaching deliberately avoids speaking of God, nevertheless on almost all levels a personal divinity (e.g., Amida Buddha), or multiple divinities or quasi-divinities (e.g., Bodhisattvas) are brought back into the de facto practice of Buddhism. An argument is made by some that such a need is simply a sign of the present immaturity of humanity, but that as it does mature, that need will disappear. Most evidence, however, seems to point in the opposite direction.

For example, immediately after the formation of the United States of America in 1789, when religious membership became completely voluntary, recorded church membership dropped to its true level of 13% of the population. But by the latter third of the twentieth century that figure had risen to over two-thirds of the population, with more than 95% expressing belief in God—and this occurred precisely during the period of the massive expansion of public education and general secularization. So, the increase of education and secularization does not appear to carry with it a necessary decrease of religious commitment and belief in God; quite the opposite happens in a genuinely free society.

d) *The Understanding of Ultimate Reality Makes a Difference*

Bearing in mind the cautions about the use of language when speaking of Ultimate Reality, I want here to probe a little further into the question I had raised before about what effect the way one conceives and speaks of Ultimate Reality has on how one acts in the world.

As noted, Christianity, as well as Judaism and Islam and some non-Semitic religions, tends to speak of Ultimate Reality in contrast to Taoism and Buddhism. The contrast is not only between personal and non-personal categories, but also between positive and negative language. In the West, Ultimate Reality is usually spoken of as Being, Fullness, *Pleroma*. In fact, the "definition" Thomas Aquinas gives for God is "Subsisting Being Itself," *Ipsum Esse Subsistens*, or in Aristotelian terms, "Pure Actuality," *Actus Purus*. As we have seen, Buddhism tends to speak of Ultimate Reality as the Void, Emptiness, *Sunyata*; in Aristotelian terms it would be "Pure Potency," *Potentia Pura*.

However, if one understands the negative terms of Buddhism not as static, mere absence of being, but as dynamic, the source of all being—as Buddhist thinkers apparently do—then the two sets of categories need not be understood as mutually contradictory, but rather, complementary, something like the two sides of a coin. They are talking about the same reality, but from two different perspectives or viewpoints. One can find such a reconciliatory position expressed by a number of Buddhist and Christian thinkers. For example, Hans Küng wrote: "Could one not, after all the explanations of emptiness . . . in comparison with the Christian understanding of the Absolute . . . also speak of *convergence between Christianity and Buddhism*?"[67]

Nevertheless, as noted, there is a huge contrast between the way the Semitic religions on the one hand and Taoism and Buddhism on the other operate in the world. The former have put massive amounts of energy into changing this world in myriad ways for the sake of the humans living in it: schools, hospitals, orphanages, social work projects, agriculture, etc., etc.

In contrast, Buddhism, and Taoism, have invested relatively very little energy in such projects. There are exceptions,

---

[67] Hans Küng, et al., *Christentum und Weltreligionen* (Munich: Piper Verlag, 1984), pp. 491f.

of course (especially in some modern Buddhist sects), and there is the Buddhist virtue of compassion and the Mahayana tradition of the Bodhisattva, one who works to help others. But the notion of ethics, especially social ethics, is largely underdeveloped in Buddhism, and, traditionally at any rate, the Bodhisattva is a rare individual, and is devoted to helping others attain *Nirvana*, rather than doing anything about changing this world. It is only the "new religions" growing out of Buddhism in the twentieth century, like Won Buddhism in Korea and Rissho Kosei-Kai in Japan, that have begun to place a stress on social ethics.

It appears to me that this major difference in how one acts "in the world" is very probably connected to the way Ultimate Reality is conceived and spoken of. Quite naturally, the positive language of "Being" is much more likely psychologically to encourage action than is the negative language of "Nothingness." Even if one can reconcile the two differing ways of conceiving and speaking so as not to be forced to make an excluding choice of one or the other, the language of one is bound to tend to generate activity and the other passivity. It must be remembered that how one conceives and speaks of Ultimate Reality provides the ultimate goal and motivation for individuals, and whole cultures, in the living of their lives. Hence, the choice of the language about Ultimate Reality is quite literally a fate-ful choice.

Therefore, Yeshua's and the whole of the Judeo-Christian-Muslim way of understanding and speaking about Ultimate Reality can, as in the past, and even more so, make an extremely positive contribution to the world of the future.

7. *Three Christian Doctrinal Problems for Moderns*

As I have already noted, modern people more and more live in a "critical-thinking" mental world, a world wherein our knowledge of the universe is increasing with a geometric acceleration in seemingly endless fashion—though that very "open-ended" knowledge also appears to be drawing in its wake an increasingly even more unfathomable "mystery." This mystery concerns not only the "whence" and "whither" of this fantastic, intricate order being revealed before our awestruck eyes, but also, and most of all, its "why?"

More and more modern people are leaving behind them the "naive" mental world in which most humans lived until not many decades ago and are moving into the second stage of maturation spoken of earlier, the "rejectionist" stage—when, e.g., the "naive" literal existence of Santa Claus is rejected. However, it is also true that an increasing number of moderns are maturing beyond the rejectionist stage to that of the "second naivete," wherein, e.g., Santa Claus is reappropriated for what he truly is, a profound symbol of a selfless concern to bring joy to others—the essence of the Christmas message.

That means that many moderns are having grave difficulties with the traditional explanations of a number of teachings that have been considered central in Christianity. This would not be the appropriate place to attempt a full scholarly analysis of all such problematic teachings. That would require a new "Summa Theologica," and I am no Thomas Aquinas—nor would my readers be so foolish as to expect a new "Summa" within the confines of a brief book.

But they can rightfully expect a few direction-pointing reflections on how at least two or three of the traditional Christian teachings that are most obviously problematic for moderns can be understood in a way compatible with the critical-thinking mentality. Furthermore, I believe that in each instance modern people will also find new light shed on these traditional teachings by entering into a dialogue with other religions which have similar teachings.

a) *Resurrection of the Body, Immortality of the Soul, Nirvana?*

Resurrection of the body (everyone's) is an article of faith that Christians have been reciting for over fifteen centuries almost every Sunday at the celebration of the Eucharist in the formula of the Nicene Creed. But of course the resurrection of the body is most of all associated with the resurrection of Jesus three days after his crucifixion.

The first thing that should be noted is that the teaching of the resurrection of the body is a peculiarly Jewish doctrine, and even more specifically, a particularly Pharisaic one. We know that the Sadducees of the time of Yeshua resisted it (operating in that case, as in many others, as a minority in the Palestinian Jewish population), but that Yeshua, and Christianity following him, along with the majority of the Jewish population, accepted it.

This fact is important to realize because the teaching of the resurrection of the body is a part of the Jewish heritage that was not suppressed in Christianity as it early passed into Hellenistic culture. This is especially striking since Christianity also accepted as its own a parallel but clearly different Hellenistic belief, namely, immortality of the soul. Of course, that teaching had already also been absorbed to some extent into Judaism by the time of Yeshua, as is witnessed to by the deuteroconical book of the "Old Testament," the Book of Wisdom (Wisdom 3:1)—but without in any way replacing the Pharisaic doctrine of the resurrection of the body.

Already at least five hundred years earlier the Greeks had developed their teaching of the immortality of the soul. For the Greeks, at least from the time of Socrates, a kind of dualism which viewed the body as the prison of the soul predominated; it was the latter, the soul, that was of true, lasting value.

Hence, in that culture, the greatest thing that could be said of one who at least some Greeks thought their greatest *hero* (Greek "Demi-god"), Socrates, was that his soul was immortal. Socrates eschewed escaping the death of the body, forced upon him in the form of the cup of hemlock, because by passing through the portals of bodily death his undying soul would return to the empyrean heavens whence it came.

The Greeks could not imagine anyone wanting to return one's incorruptible soul to the prison of one's corruptible body. St. Paul had that fact driven home to him in Athens when he held the attention of a Greek audience at the Agora when speaking of Jesus—until he began to talk of his resurrection. Then "they laughed him to scorn!" (Acts 17:32).

However, the basic Jewish understanding of humanity was that every human is a unity of an "enlivened body," a "body-soul." But the "breath of life" is something divine, coming as it did from the Creator God: "And God breathed into his nostrils the breath of life" (Genesis 2:7). Hence, since God is just, the "unnatural" state of the human body, after death, no longer being "enlivened," "ensouled," is a condition that has to be rectified—so the Jewish logic ran—and this was to be done by the "resurrection" of the body at "the end of days."

Hence, in that Jewish culture, the greatest thing that could be said of one who at least some Jews thought their greatest "hero," its Messiah (Hebrew, "Anointed One"), Yeshua ha Notzri, was that his body was "raised from the dead" by God even before the "end of days."

A simple living on of only part of God's *Imago Dei*, even though it was the spiritual part, just would not have entered the Jewish imagination as the final resolution of each human's life. In an extended sense: "What God has joined together, let no man put asunder" (Matthew 19:6).

If we look at another totally different culture we again find a different predication of its greatest "hero," Siddharta Gautama. In the Indian culture human life was seen as part of a continuum with all life. Further, there was an ineluctable structural balance built into the cosmos, called *Karma*. Hence, there developed the doctrine of "samsaric" reincarnation whereby one was constantly reborn according to the way one lived in the previous life. Thus this constant circle of reincarnation, *Samsara*, was understood in near-Sisyphean fashion, with the possibility, however, of a final break of that awful samsaric circle—called *Nirvana*.

Hence, in that Indian culture, the greatest thing that could be said of one who at least some Indians thought their greatest "hero," its *Buddha* (Sanskrit, "Enlightened One"), Siddharta Gautama, was that he had entered *Nirvana*.

Of course the Indians could not imagine that some people would want to have their body (which one!?) resurrected, or even their soul continue to live, for they understood the karmic law of the universe to have condemned them to the samsarsic circle of life until they could eventually break that ring in *Nirvana* (how that is understood varies, of course, from a variety of Hinduisms to Jainism and Buddhism, but in any case, "life" with its constant grasping for "more" was to cease).

Thus, at a very deep level what the doctrine of the resurrection of Jesus reflected was a Jewish version of the human desire to say the very best about the greatest, whether that be the immortality of the soul of Socrates, the entering into *Nirvana* of Gautama or, in this case, the bodily resurrection of Jesus. Each religious culture praised its greatest "hero" with its cultural superlative.

Now of course this is by no means all that can be said about the teaching of resurrection, or indeed of immortality or *Nirvana*. For example, bodily resurrection affirms the essential goodness of matter as well as spirit; immortality of the soul responds to the perhaps deepest of human urges, the drive for survival, and *Nirvana* answers to the profound human yearning for an endless inner peace. And much more can, and therefore should, be found in each of these doctrines. Thus this reflection is only a beginning, but I hope it can be useful at least as that.

b) *Yeshua: "God-Man" or "Human-Divine"?*

What can be said to those contemporary persons of good will and a "critical-thinking" mentality who, not ununderstandably, find talk about "God becoming Man," i.e., an Infinite-finite, literally a non-sense, a non-being, like a square circle—who point out that such contradictory words, and realities, can be placed alongside each other (e.g., a square next to a circle), but cannot be merged into a single reality? Can nothing at all be said other than: Believe! And don't ask questions!

If they still ask: Who thought up this "non-sense"? it cannot be said that Yeshua did, nor indeed that any of the biblical authors did. It must be admitted that it is the Hellenistic (mis)understanding of the typically Semitic picture-language used by Yeshua, his followers, and the biblical writers as if it were Greek ontological-language.[68]

But what of those christological dogmatic formulas hammered out in the ancient ecumenical councils to which assent was demanded under pain of excommunication? If accepted,

---

[68] For a more detailed discussion of the implications of Yeshua and his first followers' thinking and speaking Jewishly, see chapter two of my *Yeshua: A Model for Moderns* (Kansas City, MO.: Sheed & Ward, 1988).

do they not wipe out any "low Christology" (emphasizing Yeshua's humanity) and require a specific "high Christology" (emphasizing Christ's divinity), namely, according to Chalcedon (451 C.E.), that Yeshua is "truly a human being and truly God" (*vere homo et vere Deus*)? Obviously an old style catechism-like yes or no answer is not appropriate. One must first get clear about precisely what the Chalcedonian formula meant.

If taken literally, its language was, as noted, "non-sense"; it spoke of a non-thing, or no-thing, for the Council Fathers spoke of Yeshua being a "limited unlimited," a "finite infinite." But obviously they did not mean to say no-thing—even deliberately paradoxical language does not intend to communicate literal non-sense, but attempts to point to some reality beyond the apparent non-sense of the contradictory terms juxtaposed. The reader here then has the first task of discerning what meaning the authors were pointing to beyond and by way of the seeming non-sense of the juxtaposed mutually exclusive terms *homo* and *Deus*.[69]

To begin with, there is no reason to assume that the way the ancient Christian authors expressed the meaning they were attempting to communicate was necessarily the best possible, the clearest, the most helpful, etc. The very fact that the ancient Christians had to go back into council time and again over the same basic question (Nicaea, 325; Constantinople, 381; Ephesus, 431; Chalcedon, 451) amply demonstrates this point. I believe these ancient Christians were trying to express in Greek philosophical, ontological terms the Christian experience of the overwhelming confluence of the human and divine in *Yeshua ha Notzri*.

---

[69] Paul Tillich made the same point when he wrote that the statement "God has become man" is not paradoxical but "nonsensical" because "it is a combination of words which makes sense only if it is not meant to mean what the words say. The word 'God' points to ultimate reality, and even the most consistent Scotists had to admit that the only thing God cannot do is to cease to be God. But that is just what the assertion that 'God has become man' means." Paul Tillich, *Systematic Theology* (Chicago: University of Chicago, 1957), vol. 2, p. 94.

However, the ontological question was not one that excited the Semitic world. As seen, Jews tended to ask axiological rather than ontological questions: not questions of being, but of doing ("What must I *do* to gain eternal life?" not "What must I *be* or *think* to gain eternal life?" was asked of Yeshua—the Jew). This is seen reflected in the entire history and structure of Judaism; it is not the creed or doctrine that holds pride of place but the *halachah*, the rules of ethics or just action.[70]

If it is granted that the Christians meeting at Chalcedon might not have communicated their meaning in the most helpful, clearest possible language, I would then want to move from that subjunctive to the indicative mood. I am persuaded they did not express themselves as clearly, helpfully as possible for all ages to come. I would suggest that their meaning would be better expressed, today at any rate, by using adjective rather than noun forms, that is, instead of saying Yeshua is "truly a human being and truly God," *vere homo et vere Deus*, it would be clearer to say that Yeshua is "truly human and truly divine," *vere humanus et vere divinus*. The paradoxical quality of the first statement is retained in the second in that the two terms, human and divine, appear to go in opposite directions, but the juxtaposition of the two does not result in non-sense: it is con-

---

[70] A related idea about the genre of language used in various religious texts was stressed by Monika Hellwig in discussing the language of the Tome of Pope Leo the Great, which became so influential in the christological language of the Council of Chalcedon:

> Throughout this document, Leo argues directly from the language of worship and piety to the abstract formulations that came to dominate the Council of Chalcedon. There is, of course, no reflection on the nature of religious language. . . . One is compelled to ask whether there may have been a misperception of literary genre. The poetic language of piety seems to be used as though it were a simple historical record of the already self-critically nuanced language of a systematic exposition.

Monika Hellwig, "From the Jesus of Story to the Christ of Dogma," in, Alan T. Davies, ed., *Antisemitism and the Foundations of Christianity* (New York: Paulist, 1979), p. 123.

cei*vable* that someone could in some way be truly human and truly divine. In what way not only *might* this be, but in what way *was* this affirmed to be true of Yeshua?

There is no question but that not only in the earliest layers of the Christian "good news" Yeshua is portrayed as and understood to be truly human, but also even the "highest" orthodox Christian christological formulas (like that of Chalcedon) insisted on that. But, the followers of Yeshua, especially upon post-resurrection-event reflection, perceived God working in and through him in an extraordinary manner.[71] To them, God appeared to be manifesting himself through him. It seemed to them that Yeshua was so completely open to all dimensions of reality, to all being (as all human beings, as cognitive, appetitive beings, also are *in principle*), that he was totally suffused with an inpouring of "being" in a "radical," that is, in a "to the roots," way, which included the "Root," the Source of all being—in theistic language, God. Thus one could meaningfully say that Yeshua was fully, truly divine. That is, because he was fully open to all being and the Source of being there was no part of him that was not permeated with the Source of being.

It would seem that at this point many Hellenistic Christians of the patristic age made the linguistic move of saying that because Yeshua was permeated with the Source of being, with

---

[71] The Dutch Catholic theologian Ansfried Hulsbosch—who unfortunately died at a relatively young age—took the evolutionary thought of Teilhard de Chardin seriously and developed an insightful Christology. He argued that the divinity of Yeshua consisted precisely in the perfection of his humanity. He wrote that Yeshua "is the Son of God in that this man is in contact with God in a way that separates Him from ordinary men. But this can mean nothing other than a special way of being-man, since the whole actuality of the mystery lies precisely in the sector of the human." He then added that, "The divine nature of Jesus is relevant to the saving mystery only insofar as it alters and elevates the human nature. And whatever that is, it must be called a new mode of being man."

Ansfried Hulsbosch, "Jezus Christus, gekend als mens, beleden as Zoon Gods," *Tijdschrift voor Theologie*, 6 (1966), p. 255. It is summarized along with two other key articles from the same special number of the *Tijdschrift* by Piet Schoonenberg and Edward Schillebeeckx in the article "Soul-Body Unity and God-Man Unity," by Robert North in *Theological Studies*, 30 (March, 1969), pp. 27–60; 36f.

God, he therefore could also meaningfully be said to *be* truly God. But linguistically that was a confusing rather than a clarifying move because such language inadvertently also suggests that God is co-terminus with Yeshua.

That is: God is infinite, unlimited, whereas human beings, as well as all other beings, are finite, limited. However, to say that Yeshua *is* God is to say that Yeshua, a human being and therefore finite, *is* not finite, but infinite. Or, in other words: to form a sentence linking together with the nexus *is* the subject and predicate when both are nouns and at least one is exhaustive of its category can only mean that the subject and predicate are co-terminus. For example, if there is only one President of the United States, the statement that "George Bush is President" means that there is no George Bush (that particular one, who had been Vice-President) that is not President, and no President that is not George Bush; George Bush and President are limited to each other. Or: "Yeshua is God" means that there is no Yeshua that is not God and no God that is not Yeshua; Yeshua and God are limited to each other.

But that of course was not what was intended, for Christians did not wish to imply that the unlimited God was limited to Yeshua. Hence, to avoid this unintended non-sense, it would help to use the adjective form "divine" rather than the noun form "God," since the former term does not limit the Unlimited to the limited, which the latter term does.

To repeat: to say that "Yeshua is God," if both the subject and the predicate, Yeshua and God, are understood as nouns, clearly means that Yeshua and God are coextensive, that is, there is no Yeshua that is not God and there is no God that is not Yeshua. But that is obviously *not* what Christians, whether early or contemporary, mean to claim. Hence, it would appear unavoidable to conclude that in this sentence, although Yeshua is meant as a noun, God is not meant as a noun, but as an adjective. To make that clearly implied, but confusedly disguised, meaning explicitly clear, it would therefore be helpful to make the predicate specifically adjectival in form: "Yeshua is divine." Such a sentence is not non-sense and appears to capture precisely what Christians mean to say with the confusing sentence, "Yeshua is God."

i. *Prologue of John's Gospel*

But what of those passages in the New Testament itself which seem to state clearly that Yeshua is God and have been traditionally so understood, e.g., the Prologue to John's Gospel? Can they just be waved aside as the Hellenizing of the original Jewish understanding of Yeshua?

In fact, however, the New Testament, being written about, by, and for Jews, or Gentiles of a similar mentality (particularly the so-called "God-fearers" the Acts of the Apostles speaks of, that is, those Gentiles throughout the Roman Empire who attended Synagogue, followed Jewish ethics and read the "Hebrew Bible"—sort of Jewish "fellow-travelers"), did not speak of Yeshua as God. Even the passages that most readily come to mind to Christians—like John's Prologue—as without any doubt affirming that Yeshua is God, do so only if read outside of the Jewish context in which they were written. Let us take a closer look at the Prologue to John's Gospel as a prime example of, not only how much more accurate it is to understand the "problematic" New Testament texts in their Jewish context, but also how much more appropriately such an understanding fits with the modern critical-thinking, historical mentality.

> In the beginning was the Word, and the Word was with God, and the Word was God. He was in the beginning with God; all things were made through him. . . . He was in the world and the world was made by him, and the world knew him not. He came unto his own, and his own received him not. But as many as received him, to them he gave the power to become the sons of God. . . . Then I go to him who sent me (John 1:1–3, 10–12; 7:33).

Of course, if it is *assumed* ahead of time that the concept of Yeshua as the incarnation of the Second Person of the Blessed Trinity existing from all eternity could have been in the mind of the Jew John in the first century, then the words of the hymn that John recites in his Prologue can be so understood. But John wrote three hundred years before the Council at Nicaea and four hundred years before the one at Chalcedon, when this concept was hammered out—not by Jews, but by Hellenistic

Christians who were triumphant over Jews and all other religious groups in the Roman empire.

Keeping in mind, then, that here is a Jew writing largely for fellow Jews (or "fellow-travelling" God-fearers), we need to recall that there were several figures and images used in biblical and early Jewish writings as *literary images* of the invisible God as made perceivable to humans. There is the Spirit of God who already in Genesis 1:1 moves over the darkness in creation, and there is Wisdom who is present at creation (Proverbs 8:22f.; Ben Sira 24:9). In fact many scholars see the Prologue of John's Gospel as being originally largely a hymn to Wisdom, with the Word, and Jesus, being substituted by John for Wisdom. When a comparison between the Prologue and a summary of the role of Wisdom as found in Hebraic writings is made, the connection is apparent:

> Wisdom was created by God in the beginning; hidden with God and dwelling in the heavens; Wisdom was present at the Creation, in which she served as agent (or instrument); she came to earth, sent to call both Israel and all humankind, some of whom listened to her, but most of whom did not; rejected by humanity and finding no place of rest, she returned to dwell with God.[72]

There is also the image of God's Word who in numerous biblical (*Dabar*, Hebrew) and post-biblical (*Memra*, Aramaic) texts expresses God to humanity, as does God's *Torah* (Hebrew, teaching) in both biblical and post-biblical texts, as well as God's Presence (*Shekhinah*, Hebrew) in post-biblical Jewish materials. It is within the context of this plethora of Jewish imagery of God's visible side turned toward humanity that John wrote and his Jewish readers understood him. But these were all metaphors, not ontological substances, and that was likewise

---

[72] Charles E. Carlston, "Wisdom and Eschatology in Q," in "*Logia. Les paroles de Jesus—the Sayings of Jesus* in: *Bibliotheca Ephemeridum Theologicarum Lovaniensium*, 59 (Leuven: Leuven University, 1982), pp. 101f.; cited in: Ivan Havener, *Q The Sayings of Jesus* (Wilmington: Michael Glazier, 1987), p. 78.

true of John's Word, *Logos* (Greek translation—already in the Septuagint three and a half centuries before John wrote—for the Hebrew and Aramaic *Dabar*, *Memra*).

For the Jews the Word of God was God speaking: God spoke and the world was created. The Torah was God's Word —indeed the Ten Commandments, the Deca-Logue, means God's "Ten Words." God spoke to Israel through the prophets for hundreds of years. In short, the whole Jewish experience of God was God speaking, expressing Self, offering Self for a relationship with human beings. "This Self-expression of God had been going on for a long time before Jesus. It went back as far as humankind could remember. It seemed that God had always been speaking, from the beginning of the world."[73] Thus, as with Wisdom and the Spirit, it seemed to the Jews that the Word had been with God from the beginning, indeed again like Wisdom and Spirit, *was* God *as perceived by humanity*; it "expressed God's own Selfhood, and the one who encountered the word encountered God."[74]

And why did those ancient Jews see Yeshua as God's Word become flesh? Because their experience of Yeshua was that he was a diaphany of God:

> Everything God has ever said is summed up in Jesus. It is all said there, every word. Not only are the teachings of Moses and the prophets summarized in the teaching of Jesus, everything God wants to reveal about who God is is shown in who Jesus is for us. Jesus is not just someone who has occasional words to say to us on God's behalf. He is in all the dimensions of his life God's self-revelation. Thus the word of God was enfleshed in a human life. . . . This is the Johannine vision as scholars reconstruct it today.[75]

ii. *"Divinization" in Religions*

The dialogue between Christianity and Buddhism has

---

[73] Thomas N. Hart, *To Know and Follow Jesus* (New York: Paulist Press, 1984), p. 98.

[74] Ibid.

[75] Ibid., p. 99.

something to teach us Christians in the understanding of our Christologies (a Christology is simply an explanation of the meaning of Jesus the Christ). The "divinization" of the historical Yeshua into the "divine" Christ which occurred in Christianity as it moved from the Semitic cultural world into the Hellenistic was matched by a similar development with the "divinization" of the historical Siddharta Gautama into the "divine" Buddha ("Buddha," like "Christ," is not a proper name but a title; it means "the enlightened one") as it moved from the Indian cultural world into the Chinese and Far Eastern. Connected with this is the development from the "internal" understanding of "salvation," wherein each individual must strive for wholeness, to the "external," wherein help comes mainly from without. This again is like the movement from the "teaching Yeshua" to the "proclaimed Christ," from the religion *of* Yeshua to the religion *about* Yeshua the Christ, from the "Yeshua of history" to the "Christ of faith."

These shifts are also in many ways paralleled in Buddhism with the movement from the "internal" understanding of "salvation" (termed *Jiriki,* "self-power," in Japanese) to the "external" understanding (termed *Tariki,* "other power"), from the "teaching Gautama" to the "proclaimed Buddha," from the religion *of* Gautama to the religion *about* Gautama the Buddha, from "the Gautama of history" (*Shakyamuni*) to the "Buddha of belief" (*Maitreya Buddha* and *Amida Buddha*).

Seeing the same kind of developments occurring in such disparate religious cultures (one even being theistic and the other originally non-theistic) should make Christians ask themselves what deeper grasping toward an underlying insight is represented by these "divinizing" moves, these moves which "ontologized" metaphorical language. Why did Christians, Buddhists, and others, make these moves? Perhaps one way to express the deeper insight that was sought is as follows:

For Christians Yeshua is the key figure through whom they get in touch with those dimensions of reality which go beyond, which transcend the empirical, the every-day. This is fundamentally what Christologies are all about. All are attempts through the figure Yeshua to come into contact with the transcendent, the "divine," each Christology being perceived, conceived and expressed in its own cultural categories and images. Some do it better, even much better, than others; some do it even badly. Naturally they are all culture-bound. Otherwise they would not reflect and effectively speak to the people in that culture. But of course concomitantly each Christology is proportionately limited in effectiveness in regard to other cultures, whether the cultural differences result from variations in geography, time, class, or whatever.

All Christians naturally can and should learn from the insights, and failures, of all other Christians' reaching out for the transcendent in their Christologies, and other theological reflections, but what is "religiously specific" about Christians is that these Christologies, these theological reflections, are, or at least should be, intimately connected and compatible with the person Yeshua of Nazareth—though of course (!) they are not limited to imitating him in cultural detail.

However, we Christians should also be able to learn from parallel doctrines in other religious traditions. Thus, it should become clear to us Christians, and others, that in moving from talk about the "internal" to the "external," from the human to the divine, from Yeshua to Christ, we, like the Buddhists, and others, are attempting to express an experienced reality that transcends our every-day human experience, and hence also our every-day human language. We assert that there is a deeper reality which goes beyond the empirical surface experiences of our lives, and for us Yeshua is the bond-bursting means to become aware of that deeper reality (as for Buddhists it is Gautama). For us Christians it is preeminently in Yeshua that we encounter the divine, and therefore our move to talk about the divine in Yeshua. Hence, our attempt to speak of the divine in Yeshua, of Christ, etc., is not a mistake, but rather the result of the need to try to give expression to our experience with trans-empirical reality.

At the same time, however, we must be aware that when we attempt to speak of the trans-cendent we naturally will have to use trans-empirical language, that is, metaphor, symbol and the like. The mistake we must be cautious to avoid in this situation is erroneously to think that when we speak about the transcendent we are using empirical language. We are not. We can not. At the same time we must also be cautious to avoid being reductionistic and erroneously think all talk about the transcendent is merely fantasizing, that since Yeshua was merely a human being all later talk about the divine in him, etc., is simply romantic emoting with no referent in reality.

The "ontologization" move in language, that is, the "divinization" move, is then in fact a response to an experienced profound reality. It should not be dismissed, but held onto for the vital insight into the meaning of human life it strives for—but it must be correctly understood for what it is, lest it become an idol, an image falsely adored, rather than the Reality toward which it points. When it is thus correctly understood and affirmed we will then have reached Paul Ricoeur's "second naivete," the state of awareness in which the affirmation of the symbol, understood correctly for what it is, further unlocks for us the deeper, trans-empirical reality.

In sum, it must be asked: What does the Christian do about all the Christian traditions and doctrines that speak of Jesus Christ as God, the Second Person of the Blessed Trinity? They are not to be just dismissed. However, they are also not to be merely repeated with no further reflection either: simply to parrot the past is to pervert it. They must be taken with utmost seriousness, analyzed for the kind of language they are, and what reality they seek to express; they must be wrestled with and translated into our own contemporary thought categories. This is a huge task which has only been begun—and a few suggestions for which I have offered here.

c) *Ultimate Reality: One? Three? Or . . . ?*

What of the Christian teaching of the Trinity? Is it to be simply rejected as another Hellenistic misunderstanding of the Semitic picture-language? It is true that in the Hebrew Bible in addition to its insistence on monotheism ("Hear, O Israel, Yahweh our God is one." Deuteronomy 6:5) there is also much talk of God as Our Father (*Abinu*), and as we have already seen, of God's Word (*Dabar*), of God's Spirit (*Ruach*). But again, it is also equally true that these three were never thought of as ontologically existent, but rather as metaphorical images of aspects of Yahweh as encountered by the Jews.

Once again, the fact that other religious, and nonreligious, traditions likewise speak of Ultimate Reality in terms of a trinity tells us that something very deep in our human experience is being expressed in these triadic images and language.

Besides the Hebraic trinity—albeit metaphorical—an ancient form of Hinduism depicted Ultimate Reality as One in Three, the *Trimurti*: *Brahma* (a creator god, not to be confused with *Brahman*, the "Absolute" spoken of above), *Vishnu*, *Shiva*. In Mahayana Buddhism Ultimate Reality is also conceived of as triadic in the *Trikaya*, the Three-fold Body of the Buddha: *Dharma-kaya*, *Sambhoga-kaya*, *Nirmana-kaya*, as discussed earlier. Taoism also sees Ultimate Reality as triune: *T'ai I* (Grand Unity), *T'ien I* (Heavenly Unity), *Ti I* (Earthly Unity). Even in modern Western philosophy triadic thinking holds a prominent place, most evidently in Hegelian dialectical idealism and, in inverted fashion, Marxist dialectical materialism: Thesis, antithesis, synthesis. There are many other examples of the triadic view of things, but perhaps the most basically human version is the triad of man, woman, child.

In the Christian tradition there is a tendency to see the triadic form of things as reflective of the triune nature of God, epitomized in the *Imago Dei*, which naturally takes the form of the human family of man woman and child. Many modern psychologists, after Feuerbach and Freud, would tend to say that rather than humanity reflecting the nature of God, the human description of God is a projection of human experience. Humanity is not an *Imago Dei*, but God is an *Imago hominis*.

Again, however, one does not need to make a choice. Both could well be understood as true—indeed as mutually necessary, though for asymmetrical reasons. Of course humans speak of Ultimate Reality, of God, in human terms. What alternatives are there? To be sure, as noted before, Ultimate Reality can be spoken of in impersonal terms. But to many this seems all right, but too little—on the principle of sufficient reason: Ultimate Reality must be at least as perfect as the most perfect finite being, so therefore at least "personal," though without the limitations we see in limited human persons. It also seems logical that the effect will be a reflection of its cause: e.g., If there are only blond genes in both parents, it is expected the offspring will be blond; conversely, blond offspring imply blond genes in the parents.

So, it is "natural" that Christians, along with many other religious persons, perceive Ultimate Reality as somehow triadic, thereby giving rise to the doctrine of the Trinity: One God in three divine persons. Given the early move of Christianity into the Hellenist thought world, it is not at all surprising that the prominent Jewish triadic imagery would give rise to the more philosophical reflections that developed the doctrine of the triune God. This is especially true since the teaching of the *Imago Dei* was also so strong in Judaism.

For there is not only the fundamental physical triad in human biology (and in all higher animal biology), but, perhaps even more importantly, also in human psychology, wherein the quality of being a divine image is thought to reside mainly: Knowing the true, loving the good, acting freely. Long before Martin Buber, Christians were aware that the human "I-thou" relationship is qualitatively far beyond an "I-it" relationship. One of the special characteristics about an I-thou relationship is that it creates a third reality: I am aware of (love) you; you are aware of (love) me; we are aware that we are aware of (love) each other. The relationship between the I and the thou becomes a third reality, as it does not in an I-it relationship. This human psychological triad is mirrored at its zenith in the mutual love between a woman and a man resulting in a third reality, a third person, the child.

This rather universal human experience of a mutual awareness (love) creating a third reality between persons gave rise to the development of the renowned attempt by St. Augustine to "explain" the Trinity in psychological terms: God the Father expresses himself completely (the Word); in mutually contemplating complete perfection in each other, the Father and his Word love each other completely; since this mutual love is perfect, it also is a third reality, called the Spirit.

Whether one finds such an "explanation" very helpful or not, it should be apparent that the Christian doctrine of the

Trinity—however it is "explained," whether in Augustine's psychological terms, the Council of Chalcedon's Greek philosophical categories, or whatever—is an attempt, like the triadic doctrines of the other religions and philosophies, to point to a basic trinitarian form of reality, both finite and infinite.

To repeat what has been said above: These are three attempts to try to "make sense" in contemporary thought categories out of three representative traditional Christian doctrines which have become problematic for critical-thinking moderns.

8. *Dialogue: A Key to the Future*

a) *Yeshua's Attitude Toward Non-Jews*

One would not usually think of Yeshua in connection with interreligious dialogue. On the one hand he is recorded to have sent out the twelve apostles only "to the lost sheep of the people of Israel" (Matthew 10:6). On the other, he is also recorded to have said to them that they "should tell the Good News to the Gentiles" (Matthew 10:18), and "the Good News must be preached to all nations" (Mark 13:10). Moreover, Yeshua himself did go into the Gentile area of present-day Lebanon.

There is also clear evidence of an openness on his part to the Gentiles: When he was accosted by a Roman officer for help for his servant, Yeshua was shaken and said, "I have never found anyone in Israel with faith like this!" (Matthew 8:10). When Yeshua was in the Gentile country around Tyre and Sidon a Canaanite woman pleaded with him to help her afflicted daughter, he at first ignored her, then said that he was "sent only to the lost sheep of the people of Israel." She persisted, however, in an even brash manner. Yeshua was obviously stunned, and having been confronted with his narrow nationalistic view by this pagan woman, he relented and complied with her request.

Much more evidence than this we do not have, largely because the life of Yeshua was brutally cut short early in his manhood, thirty to thirty-three years old. That this is all the evidence we have is also due to the fact that his followers were obviously bent upon spreading his "Good News," and were not particularly interested in his attitude toward other religions. However, we can draw some probable conclusions both from the evidence above of Yeshua's openness to Gentiles (not all Jewish schools of that time were open to the value of Gentiles —e.g., the then dominant school of Pharisees, the Shammaites, despised Gentiles) and the fact that his followers almost immediately moved into Gentile areas. Thus, there was clearly a universalist quality about the attitude of Yeshua and his followers —which reflected the long-existing universalistic strand in Judaism.

How this attitude would have developed had Yeshua lived a few decades longer, or what his response would have been had he then encountered a profound devotee of Buddhism (there is evidence that there were Buddhists in the Near East around that time), is something that one can only muse about: If the trajectory of an openness to learning from those of other religions evidenced in the scraps of Gospel evidence we have held true to course, the world would probably have been the beneficiary of a profound religious dialogue that we are only beginning to approximate today.

b) *Meaning and Implications of Dialogue Today*

One of the most dramatic elements of today's paradigm shift is the radical reversal by the majority of Christianity away from an imperialistic debate-oriented stance toward non-Christians to a dialogue-oriented one. This can be seen on all levels, scholarly, grass-roots and institutional—the latter, for example, in a number of official documents from various Protestant denominations, but in its most influential form in the documents of the Catholic Church at Vatican Council II (1962–65) and subsequently.

The Council stated that "Catholics are to be keen on collaborating with all men of good will. . . . They are to enter into dialogue with them, approaching them with understanding and courtesy."[76] In his very first encyclical (1964), Pope Paul VI

[76] Vatican II, *Decree on the Apostolate of the Laity*, number 14.

wrote: "Dialogue is demanded nowadays. . . . It is demanded . . . by the maturity man has reached in this day and age."[77] In 1968 the Vatican Secretariat for Dialogue with Unbelievers wrote that, "Doctrinal dialogue should be initiated with courage and sincerity, with the greatest freedom," and added these stunning words: "Doctrinal discussion [must] recognize the truth everywhere, even if the truth demolishes one so that one is forced to reconsider one's own position, in theory and in practice."[78]

This is not the place to repeat my earlier reflections on interreligious, interideological dialogue.[79] However, it should be recalled that interreligious dialogue essentially is a conversation with someone of a different religion (or ideology), the *primary* purpose of which is for me to learn—not teach. Such an action presumes that both partners have what I termed above a "deabsolutized" understanding of truth. That is, they are convinced that their understanding and description of reality—truth—is correct, but always limited (in that sense, "deabsolutized"); hence they have something to learn about reality from persons who perceive it differently. From this it follows that dialogue is not only permissible, but even mandatory if I wish to learn ever more about reality—which every religious person, indeed, every human, by nature wishes to do.

Dialogue as a key to an ever expanding future of deepening knowledge of reality, including Ultimate Reality, is an insight that is sweeping through Christianity, and through it into all the religions and ideologies of the world. It is creatively transforming Christianity, and will do so even more profoundly in the future.

---

[77] Pope Paul VI's encyclical *Ecclesiam suam*, 1964, number 79.

[78] *Humanae personae dignitatem*, August 28, 1968, Austin Flannery, ed., *Vatican Council II* (Collegeville, MN: Liturgical Press, 1975), pp. 1007, 1010.

[79] See, for example, the *Journal of Ecumenical Studies*, which my wife Arlene Anderson Swidler and I founded in 1964 and which I edit; Leonard Swidler, John Cobb, Jr., Paul Knitter, Monika Hellwig, *Death or Dialogue? From the Age of Monologue to the Age of Dialogue* (Philadelphia: Trinity, 1990); Leonard Swidler, *After the Absolute. The Dialogical Future of Religious Reflection* (Minneapolis: Fortress, 1990).

Thus, Christianity has two unique gifts to offer the world in the Third Millennium, one formal and one substantive and personal. The first is "Dialogue," the key to a never-ending creative future, and in that dialogue, Christianity's always vital and vitalizing Source: Yeshua.

V. FINAL CONCLUSION

The basic drive for physical survival is something humanity shares with the other living beings, but it is not what makes women and men human. Humans are beings who can know and love and act freely with knowledge. In fact, humans not only can, but also must, know and love and act freely with knowledge if they are to be something more than beasts, if they are to be at all human. But once humans have started on the path of knowing and loving and acting freely with knowledge they will not be satisfied with knowing and loving and freely acting knowingly just a little, or even a lot. Human nature is directed at an open-ended, endless, in-finite, all-embracing, comprehensive knowing and loving and knowing freely acting. That total knowing and loving and knowing freely acting that humans, both individually and communally, have created over the centuries is Religion, and the Culture that matches it.

In the past, individuals and their various cultures have tended to live in relative isolation from each other; only a few extraordinary individuals truly crossed over into alien cultures. But such isolation is no longer possible in the world at the edge of the Third Millennium. Although cultures remain distinct, they can no longer remain untouched by others. All of our different cultures must now live within a Global Culture.

The situation is similar for religions. Several of the world religions and ideologies have attempted to dominate the world, and four of them have had rather remarkable success: Buddhism, Christianity, Islam and Marxism. Only the first never tried to expand by the force of arms; it took the path of a "passive imperialism." The other three tried the "aggressive imperialist" approach. But it is clear from experience that no one of these, or any other, religion/ideology will be completely triumphant and destroy all the rest. Rather, just as the various cultures of the world must now live within a Global Culture, so also the religions of the world must now live within a Global Dialogue.

It is the unique human breakthrough to an open-ended economic, scientific, political progress of Western civilization that has brought the world to the necessity of a Global Culture. Christianity as the major religion of Western civilization has correspondingly brought the world to the necessity of a Global Dialogue.

Leading the way into that dialogue is Christianity's formal contribution to the world of the Third Millennium. Christianity has many valuable substantive contributions to make to the world in this dialogue, but by far its most important, and its unique contribution is its newly available Source: Yeshua of Nazareth.